Studien zur Mustererkennung

herausgegeben von:

Prof. Dr.-Ing. Heinrich Niemann

Prof. Dr.-Ing. Elmar Nöth

Bibliografische Information der Deutschen Nationalbibliothek

Die Deutsche Nationalbibliothek verzeichnet diese Publikation in der Deutschen Nationalbibliografie; detaillierte bibliografische Daten sind im Internet über http://dnb.d-nb.de abrufbar.

ISBN 978-3-8325-4807-0
ISSN 1617-0695

Logos Verlag Berlin GmbH
Comeniushof
Gubener Str. 47
10243 Berlin
Tel.: +49 030 42 85 10 90
Fax: +49 030 42 85 10 92
INTERNET: http://www.logos-verlag.de

Human Activity Analysis in Visual Surveillance and Healthcare

DISSERTATION

zur Erlangung des Grades eines Doktors
der Ingenieurwissenschaften

vorgelegt von
M.Sc. Muhammad Hassan Khan
geb. am 02.09.1983 in Pakistan.

eingereicht bei der Naturwissenschaftlich-Technischen Fakultät
der Universität Siegen
Siegen 2018

Gutachter der Dissertation:

1. Prof. Dr. Marcin Grzegorzek

2. Prof. Dr. Frank Deinzer
(Hochschule für angewandte Wissenschaften Würzburg-Schweinfurt)

Tag der mündlichen Prüfung:

13. September 2018.

Acknowledgements

I would like to express my sincere gratitude to all the people, without whom, the pursuit of my doctoral studies would not have been possible. First and foremost, I would like to express my special appreciations and thanks to my supervisor Prof. Marcin Grzegorzek for his everlasting encouragement, optimism and belief in me. His consistent guidance, untiring effort and incredible support from the first day of my doctoral studies helped me in all the time of research and writing of this thesis. Without his great supervisory, my doctoral research would not have seen the light of the day. I would like to extend my thanks to Prof. Frank Deinzer who agreed to be my second supervisor as well as Prof. Roland Wismüller, Prof. Michael Möller and Prof. Markus Lohrey for being their acceptance to serve in my examination committee. I am very thankful for their positive comments and invaluable discussion regarding my work.

I would like to express my special gratitude to Dr. Muhammad Shahid Farid and Dr. Kimiaki Shirahama for their continuous help, academic guidance and constructive persuading throughout my PhD. My gratitude is extended to all the members and alumni of the Research Group for Pattern Recognition at University of Siegen, for being professional colleagues and great friends. I am very glad to have known you and really appreciate working with you. I would also like to thank my friends in Germany whom I had a wonderful time with and friends in Pakistan who share my failures and successes. I am also thankful to University of the Punjab, Pakistan for providing a financial support to pursue my doctoral studies. In particular, I would like to thank Prof. Syed Mansoor Sarwar for his helpful advices and kind attitude.

Last but not least, my special appreciation goes to my parents for encouraging me to pursue my interest and supporting me spiritually throughout the doctoral studies and my life in general. I am thankful to my brothers and sisters for their loving support. Finally, my heartfelt gratitude goes to my wife Ammara due to her patience and constant inspiring encouragement; and to my children Ayesha, Umer and Arham whom I could not being engaged with as expected. Thank you for all the joy and support and many memorable moments staying in Germany with you.

Abstract

Human activity analysis has received significant research attention in the recent years due to its applications in several fields such as monitoring, healthcare, surveillance, and entertainment. Human activities range from simple gestures *e.g.* hand-shaking, to the complex movements involving whole body *e.g.* walking; and they are usually captured with video cameras and motion sensors. This dissertation presents novel techniques for human activity analysis in a visual surveillance scenario and also proposes a smart healthcare system to monitor the human well-being using video data.

Biometric modalities have emerged as reliable means in recognizing the individuals using their physiological and behavioral characteristics. Gait is considered as an important biometric feature and it refers to the walking style of human. Unlike other physiological biometric modalities such as fingerprint, face, iris; gait does not require human interaction with the imaging system. Moreover, it can be collected at low-resolution in a non-invasive and hidden manner. In the last couple of decades, gait recognition has received significant attention due to its promising performance in a controlled environment. However, the recent research is more focused on gait recognition in realistic environment where it is necessary to deal with the variations in gait patterns due to the change in viewing angle, carrying goods during the walk, walking-surface, clothing, *etc*. The first part of this dissertation proposes a novel gait descriptor which effectively meets these challenges and can be assistive in the development of better surveillance systems. The proposed descriptor is based on the spatial and the temporal motion characteristics of human walk. It offers an efficient representation of gait for a person identification. Unlike most existing gait recognition algorithms which construct the gait descriptors using the segmented human body region from the video, the proposed gait representation is segmentation free. Moreover, it is extended to solve the problem of cross-view gait recognition using a deep neural network.

Movement analysis of human body parts is a fundamental step for many applications such as the detection of infantile movement disorders, analyzing the performance of athletes, and activity detection. Existing techniques are either marker-based solutions or they use wearable motion sensors to analyze the movements. The second part of this dissertation proposes a smart healthcare system to analyze the movements of human body parts by using only the video data, without adopting any wearable sensors or markers. The aim of the proposed system is the early detection of movement disorders, and the assessment of human's action during the therapeutic treatment. In particular, two methods are proposed to analyze the movement patterns in human body. The first method detects the human body parts and tracks them temporally to encode the respective motion information. The second algorithm exploits geometrical configurations of human body parts to detect their movements.

The proposed techniques are evaluated on the benchmark datasets and the results are compared with the state-of-the-art methods to prove their effectiveness.

Zusammenfassung

Die Analyse der Aktivitäten des Menschen war in den vergangenen Jahren Ziel erheblicher Forschungsbemühungen aufgrund ihrer Anwendungen in verschiedenen Bereichen wie Beobachtung, Gesundheitspflege, Überwachung oder Unterhaltung. Menschliche Aktivitäten reichen von einfachen Gesten, wie beispielsweise Händeschütteln, bis hin zu komplexen Bewegungen, die den gesamten Körper beanspruchen, wie zum Beispiel Gehen, und werden häufig mithilfe von Videokameras und Bewegungssensoren erfasst. Diese Doktorarbeit präsentiert neuartige Techniken zur Analyse menschlicher Aktivitäten in visuellen Überwachungssystemen und schlägt ein intelligentes System zur Gesundheitspflege vor, welches das Wohlergehen des Menschen mithilfe von Videodaten beobachtet.

Biometrische Modalitäten haben sich als eine zuverlässige Weise Individuen zu erkennen herausgebildet, indem sie von physiologischen und verhaltensbezogenen Charakteristiken Gebrauch machen. In dieser Hinsicht gilt die Gangart des Menschen als wichtiges biometrisches Merkmal. Sie verlangt, im Gegensatz zu anderen physiologisch-biometrischen Modalitäten wie dem Fingerabdruck, dem Gesicht oder der Iris, keine Interaktion des Menschen mit dem Bildgebungssystem. Zudem kann die Gangart mit geringer Auflösung und auf nicht-invasive und versteckte Weise erfasst werden. In den letzten Jahrzehnten wurde der Erkennung der Gangart eine signifikante Aufmerksamkeit zuteil, dies geschah aufgrund ihrer vielversprechenden Leistung in kontrollierten Umgebungen. Jüngste Forschungsbemühungen konzentrieren sich jedoch mehr auf die Erkennung der Gangart in einer realistischen Umgebung, in der es notwendig ist, sich mit Abweichungen im Muster des Gangs zu beschäftigen, ausgelöst beispielsweise durch einen sich ändernden Blickwinkel, durch Gegenstände, die währenddessen getragen werden, durch den Untergrund, auf dem man sich bewegt, oder die Kleidung, die man trägt, *etc.* Der erste Teil dieser Arbeit stellt einen neuen Gangart-Deskriptor vor, der sich diesen Herausforderungen stellt und bei der Entwicklung besserer Überwachungssysteme nützlich sein kann. Dieser Deskriptor basiert auf den räumlichen und zeitlichen Charakteristiken des menschlichen Gangs. Er bietet eine effiziente Repräsentation der Gangart zur Identifizierung von Personen. Im Gegensatz zu den meisten bereits existierenden Gangerkennungsalgorithmen, die

Gangart-Deskriptoren erzeugen, indem sie die menschliche Körperregion aus dem Video segmentieren,benötigt der vorgestellte Gangart-Deskriptor keine Segmentierung. Er wurde außerdem erweitert, um das Problem der Gangart-Erkennung bei Queransicht mithilfe eines tiefen neuralen Netzwerks zu lösen.

Die Bewegungsanalyse menschlicher Körperteile ist ein fundamentaler Schritt in vielen Anwendungen, wie in der Erkennung von Bewegungsstörungen im Kindesalter, der Leistungsanalyse von Athleten oder der Aktivitätserkennung. Existierende Lösungen basieren entweder auf der Verwendung von Markierungen oder nutzen tragbare Bewegungssensoren zur Bewegungsanalyse. Der zweite Teil dieser Doktorarbeit stellt ein intelligentes System zur Gesundheitspflege zur Erkennung von Bewegungen in menschlichen Körperteilen auf Basis von Videodaten und ohne Verwendung von tragbaren Sensoren oder Markierungen vor. Ziel dieses Systems ist die frühe Erkennung von Bewegungsstörungen und die Bewertung menschlichen Verhaltens während der therapeutischen Behandlung. Insbesondere werden zwei Methoden vorgestellt, welche die Bewegungsmuster im menschlichen Körper analysieren. Die erste dieser Methoden erkennt die Körperteile des Menschen und verfolgt sie zeitlich zur Kodierung der Bewegungsinformation. Der zweite Algorithmus macht sich geometrische Beschaffenheiten der einzelnen Körperteile des Menschen zunutze, um ihre Bewegung zu erkennen.

Die dargebotenen Techniken werden auf Benchmark-Datensets angewandt und bewertet, und die Ergebnisse werden mit den neuesten Techniken verglichen, um ihre Effektivität zu beweisen.

Contents

Chapter 1

Introduction

The aim of vision-based human activity recognition is to automatically analyze the ongoing actions in a video. Generally, these activities are recorded using a visual sensor (*e.g.* standard colour camera, multi-view camera setup or Time-of-Flight (TOF) camera). Based upon the complexity, the activities can be divided into four categories, namely gesture, action, interaction and group activity [AR11]. A gesture is an elementary movement in a human body part describing the meaningful motion of the human such as raising a leg, stretching an arm, *etc.* The combination of temporally organized gestures in one person is known as an action. Examples of action include walking, running, jumping. Interactions are performed by two actors, where one must be a human and the second may be a human or an object, such as a therapy process given to the patient by the therapist, person using a computer, *etc.* Whereas the group activity consists of multiple subjects and objects with a various combination of gestures, actions, and interactions *e.g.* a group of people marching, dancing or having a meeting. An automatic recognition of human activities in video data enables their use in several applications such as assisted living [Che+11], clinical assessment [CCH11], rehabilitation places [Wu11], gesture-based interactive games [Eve+11], physical therapy [PD13], and visual surveillance [Bou+11]. The activities focused in this dissertation belong to the gestures and actions, with applications in visual surveillance, biometric authentication, movement disorders, and evaluation of therapeutic procedure.

Person identification is an active research area due to its importance for individual authentication in many advanced applications such as surveillance, forensic, and access control. Unlike traditional methods of authentication which use password and PIN (personal identification number) code, the biometric has gained a widespread acceptance in computer-vision based applications to provide the legitimate authentication of identity for an individual [O'G03]. It refers to the recognition of an individual using his/her physiological and behavioral characteristics. The physiological traits of a human which may consists of

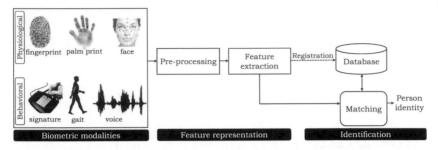

Figure 1.1: Framework of a biometric based authentication system.

fingerprint, DNA, palm print, face, iris; whereas the behavioral characteristics may include gait, voice, signature, typing rhythm have been proven as a source of person identification in many systems [Zha12]. To validate the identity of an individual, biometric based authentication systems extract the required features from the given modality and measure the similarity with the already registered features in the database as illustrated in Figure 1.1.

Amongst the biometric modalities, gait has a unique advantage due to its ability to recognize an individual at distance, in low-resolution video, and without making any interaction with the system. Gait refers to the walking style of a person and can be defined as *the coordinated, cyclic combination of movements that result in human locomotion* [BL05]. Movement coordination means that they must occur in a specific temporal pattern, whereas cyclic represents the repetition of steps between the alternating feet. Gait is the composition of both coordinated and cyclic nature of the human motion and their static shape. Although these movement patterns in humans look similar, they are different in the underlying kinematics of gait such as their relative timing and magnitudes [BCD02]. Several features such as physical length of human body parts, stride-length, and speed contribute in constructing a gait representation. In recent years, due to extensive usage of closed-circuit television (CCTV) cameras in public places such as airports, banks, government buildings and in the restricted access area, for example military-depots and data access centers; person identification at distance may play an important role for crime prevention and forensic identification. The report published in [Bar13] has shown that the British Security Industry Authority has estimated that more than 5.9 million CCTV cameras are mounted for surveillance in nationwide. To efficiently supervise this huge amount of CCTVs data, the need of intelligent visual surveillance systems is acute. Person identification using gait has already contributed to evidence collection for convicting criminal activities such as bank robbery in Denmark [LSL08] and the recognition of burglar in United Kingdom [Bou+11]. In addition to surveillance applications, gait has also been employed at several clinical and rehabilitation places, *e.g.*

(a)   (b)

Figure 1.2: Example of movement analysis of human body parts: (a) therapy treatment [DD], and (b) athlete's bowling action [RL14].

to estimate the gait abnormalities in patients affected by Parkinson's disease [Pra+11], to predict the fall detection [Rou+07] and analysis of gait in rehabilitation process [ZTB16]. The first part of this dissertation presents novel algorithms to identify an individual by his/her gait.

Although gait is not as powerful as other physiological biometric modalities, its characteristics to recognize a person at distance and without making any interaction with the system make it irreplaceable in may applications, particularly in visual surveillance. Moreover, it can be collected in a hidden manner without alerting the individuals. However, vision-based gait recognition suffers from a few challenges because many factors may affect it, such as variations in clothing, walking speed, walking surface, footwear, carrying objects, viewing angle, injuries and others.

An automatic analysis of human body parts' movements is a highly active research area because of its several computer-vision based applications and its inherent complexity. These movements are usually computed by localizing the different body parts and their tracking in temporal domain [AC99]. Such an analysis is extremely useful in several applications *e.g.* to analyze the performance of athletes, clinical diagnostics and assessment systems, as illustrated in Figure 1.2. Moreover, the movement analysis of human body parts further leads to analyze the human activities in many advanced applications such as human-robot interaction, automatic control of airbags and sleep detection during the driving. Since the human body is consist of several parts connected at joints and posses the high degree of articulation, due to the non-rigid nature of these parts, the detection and tracking across the frames in a video is the most challenging task. The second part of this dissertation lays emphasis on the movement analysis of different body parts in human, which may help in the clinical assessment to detect any movement disorders and the evaluation of the desired therapeutic program.

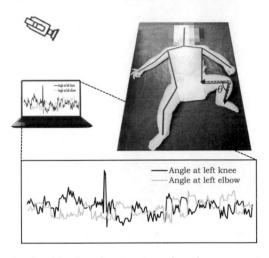

Figure 1.3: Example of a vision-based system to analyze the movements of infant's body parts.

The normal human movements such as waving an arm and moving a leg seem to be simple, but they require a complex coordination of control between the brain and musculoskeletal system. Any interruption in the coordination system may cause an inhabit undesired movement, problems in making the desired movement or both [Min96]. These movement abnormalities are known as *movement disorders* which may appear due to the abnormal development of the brain, injury in the brain of a child during pregnancy or at birth, and genetic disorders. Consequently, they introduce movement disorders in the newborn, *e.g.* cerebral palsy, spinal scoliosis, peripheral paralysis of arms/legs, hip joint dysplasia and various myopathies. Numerous studies [Gro+05; Pie02; Mei+06; Sta+12] have shown that the early detection of movement disorders plays an important role in the early intervention and building a desired therapy program to follow-up. To diagnose the movement disorders in children, the professional personnel, often doctors or physiotherapists, observe the spontaneous movements of different body parts along with other factors such as family history. This examination is known as *General Movement Assessment (GMA)* [Pre01]. However, it is a subjective procedure based on observer's expertise and does not have any standardized criteria to quantify the results. Furthermore, it is a tedious procedure to manually analyze every infant. Therefore, the need of an automatic system to analyze such movements in a human body region is acute to help the clinicians in their work. Figure 1.3 presents an example of a vision-based system to analyze the movements of different body parts.

The analysis of human activities spans over an enormous number of activity patterns; however, this dissertation focuses on two areas: person identification in visual surveillance and the movement analysis of human body parts in the clinical assessment and evaluation systems. More specifically, this work aims (1) to recognize the person identity using gait in realistic scenarios, (2) to analyze the movement patterns in different body parts to detect any movement disorders, and (3) to evaluate the therapeutic procedures.

1.1 Problem

Person identification using gait is a challenging task as the walk patterns in humans look very similar. Moreover, the gait is often degraded by many covariate factors such as clothing styles, carrying objects during the walk, change in walking surface, walk speed, footwear, viewing angle, injuries, *etc*. Usually, the gait is collected at distance, in low resolution and without alerting the subject. The automatic gait recognition system extracts the gait features from the video sequence and uses them to measure their similarity with the existing ones through a pre-defined matching mechanism.

The existing gait recognition techniques can be categorized into two approaches: model-based[Wan+04; CNC03; AN12] and appearance-based [HB06; Wan+12; YTL14]. The model-based approaches use the human body structure and motion models in the gait sequence to identify an individual. They characterize a human subject using a structural model and track several body parts and joint positions over time to describe the gait. Specifically, the human body region is modeled using the underlying mathematical structure, *e.g.* stick-figure [AN12], interlinked pendulum [CNC03] and ellipse fitting techniques [LG02]; and the motion parameters of the subject, *e.g.* joint angle trajectories [Wan+04], rotation patterns of hip and thigh [CNC03] are used to recognize a person. Few examples of model-based gait extraction are shown in Figure 1.4a – 1.4b. It can be seen that the computation of such parameters requires the localization of the torso which is quite difficult from the low-resolution images, captured at distance in real surveillance systems. The model-based gait recognition approaches are computationally expensive and sensitive to video quality [YTL14].

Contrastingly, the appearance-based approaches operate on the captured images directly. The majority of such approaches extract the human body region from the images and construct a gait representation using the spatiotemporal shape and the dynamic motion characteristics. Few model-free gait representations are shown in Figure 1.4c – 1.4d, where the information of human body region is segmented from the background and averaged over a gait-cycle. Although the appearance-based approaches are considered efficient, the recognition accuracy of such approaches is dependent on the precise segmented shape of

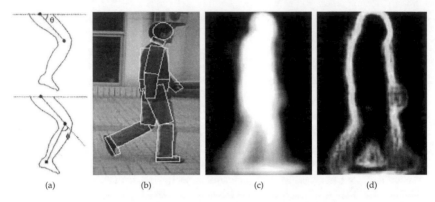

(a)　　　　　　　　(b)　　　　　　　　(c)　　　　　　　　(d)

Figure 1.4: Example of model-based and appearance-based gait representations. (a)-(b) Model-based [CNC03; Wan+04], and (c)-(d) appearance-based [HB06; Wan+12].

human body which is still a challenging problem in the literature. An inaccurate segmentation may lower the recognition accuracy [ZWY14]. Thus, the need of a more accurate gait representation that can deal with all these challenges is momentous.

Among the aforementioned covariate factors, viewing angle is the most challenging and unavoidable aspect in the real world visual surveillance systems. The appearance changes in a person's walk due to change in the viewing angle introduce intra-personal variations which are always larger than inter-personal variations caused by the other covariates. In real world surveillance systems, usually the CCTVs are mounted at different positions and altitudes. Moreover, the direction of an individual's walk is also dependent on his/her destination. Due to these factors, the variations in the appearance of a person's walk alter the gait representation significantly. Therefore, it is required to normalize the appearance based two dimensional (2D) gait representation prior to measure their similarities across the viewpoints. To cope with this problem, a three dimensional (3D) prospective of the person's walk using multi-camera setup is one of the possible solutions and it can be employed to accurately construct the 3D representation of the walk. However, such scenarios are only applicable in a fully controlled and calibrated multi-camera environment, which is costly and requires expensive computation. On the contrary, TOF cameras such as Microsoft Kinect provide the depth information which can be used to build a 3D representation of the gait. In addition to their high accuracy [Kha+16c], they are cheap and easy to use as well. However, despite these advantages, the restrictions of depth cameras (*e.g.* small depth range) make their applicability for visual surveillance very limited. Therefore, the majority of the visual sensors used in real surveillance systems are monocular cameras which are cheap, easy to use and do not require any calibration. Regardless of which visual sensors were used in the recording; the gait representation must be generic and view-invariant to deal with all these challenges. To cope with all these challenges, a novel gait representation is proposed in the first part of this dissertation. The proposed representation does not involve any human body segmentation from the images. It aims to build a high-level gait representation using the spatial and temporal motion information extracted from the video sequence of the walk. Furthermore, the proposed representation is extended to construct its view-invariant gait representation. The proposed algorithms achieved excellent results in both the single-view and the cross-view gait recognition.

The challenge of automatically analyzing the movements of human body parts lie on several difficulties. First, the localization of the desired body part in images/video where the movements need to be analyzed. Since they are characterized by diverse visual appearances and locations in the image, they require an exhaustive search to detect each body part in all possible regions of the image. To avoid these heavy computations, it is necessary to restrict the search area in the image to the region that most likely contains the desired object. Second, the problem in detecting the body parts is their movements, which may results in a tremendous amount of body part's shapes due to large degree of freedom in the articulation of several parts. The other problems which may also affect the appearance of body parts include the colour, clothing, illumination, *etc.* The detected body parts location is used to estimate the joints, and their tracking in temporal domain encodes the motion information. Additionally, colour or infrared based markers are another mean to efficiently detect and track the body parts in visual data without employing any exhaustive search. The body parts are detected using the calibration process of markers and their tracking in successive frames encode the motion. However, they require extra hardware attached to the human body and the complex calibration process [DG+12].

Rather than visual data, wearable motion sensor such as Inertial Measurement Units (IMU) have also been exploited to assess the motion information in different body parts and perform a quantitative analysis. An IMU is the combination of gyroscopes, accelerometers and magnetometers. It provides the motion information relevant to angular velocity and acceleration in the sensor/body, and the magnetic field around it [Ble+13]. Figure 1.5a illustrates the idea of using accelerators to capture the motion information at different limbs. However, wearing the sensors or markers on the human body may cause discomfort to the patients, especially to the young babies [Kha+16b] and may affect on their natural movements. Visual 3D sensor such as Microsoft Kinect is another mean to detect different body parts and the analysis of their movements (Figure 1.5b). It has been used in conjunction with its depth information [Hes+15], integrated body tracking functionality [Exe+13] and

(a)   (b)

Figure 1.5: Example of movement analysis of different body parts. (a) Using motion sensors [Hei+10] and (b) visual sensor with tracking functionality.

body part model fitting techniques [Ols+14; Kha+16a] to segment and encode the motion information in different body parts. Despite the fact that the invention of the Kinect sensor has prompted the interest of the research community in building numerous applications on human motion analysis for rehabilitation and clinical assessment, its limitation of 1 meter on the size of the subject for integrated body tracking prevents it's use in the detection and movement analysis of infants. Moreover, they suffer with the limitation of sensor's range.

In the second part of this dissertation, vision-based methods are proposed to automatically detect and track the movements of different body parts. Furthermore, the motion information has been employed in two different clinical applications: (1) in an assessment of movement disorders in human body parts; (2) in evaluation of the therapeutic procedure. In particular, the objective is to accurately detect the all body parts without using any markers or sensors. Based on the body part detection, the motion information at different joints is encoded in temporal domain and is efficiently used in these applications.

1.2 Contribution

There are two major contributions of this dissertation. First, to exploit an individual's walk pattern to recognize his/her identity in visual surveillance and forensic systems. For this purpose, the overall motion patterns of walk are extracted directly from the video sequence and a novel gait representation is proposed which is able to deal with all challenges described in the previous section. Second, proposal of novel algorithms for the detection and the movement analysis of human body parts, and their use in the clinical assessment and evaluation applications. The contributions of this dissertation are summarized in the following:

- **Spatiotemporal Gait Representation:** Most existing gait recognition approaches build a gait representation using the segmented human body region from the images/video. The most simple and well-known technique in this regard is gait energy image (GEI) [HB06] which has been widely used in gait recognition algorithms due to its effectiveness and simplicity in the implementation. This gait representation is based on a template image which is obtained by segmenting the human body region (*i.e.,* silhouette shape) from the images/video through background modeling, and they are normalized and averaged over the gait-cycle. The template images of walking persons are then used to measure their similarities. Rather than creating a template image, the authors in [ZWY14] computed several statistical measurements from the segmented silhouette shape over the time such as the height and width ratio and centroid of the contour; and used them to recognize the gait through Radial Basis Function (RBF) network and deterministic learning. One can observe that the recognition performance of such techniques may degrade heavily if the segmented shape is not accurate. In order to cope this problem, two methods are proposed to build a gait representation based on the spatial and the temporal motion characteristics of human walk. Both proposed algorithms do not require any segmentation or gait-cycle estimation, and can be computed directly from the video sequences. The experimental evaluations conducted on five large benchmark gait databases confirm the effectiveness of the proposed gait recognition techniques.

- **View-invariant Gait Recognition:** Usually, the 2D gait representations are not robust to the variations in the appearance of gait caused by the change in viewing angle. The existing studies *e.g.* [WRB06] show that the performance of single-view based recognition method on video related tasks may drop up-to 60%, when they are used for cross-view recognition without normalizing the effect of variations due to change in the viewing-angle. To solve this problem, the researchers in [Bod+09; LF+16; Tan+17] proposed to construct a 3D human model and derived several features such as the length of body segments and angular data of the subject's movement, using multi-view synchronized images. However, these techniques require an expensive setup of multiple calibrated cameras and can only work in a well-controlled environment. Conversely, the view transformation model (VTM)-based approaches *e.g.* [BXG10a; Kus+14; Mak+06; Kus+09b] learn a mapping/transformation between the gait descriptors obtained from different viewpoints. Usually, the learning process of such techniques is based on view-pairs, appearing in the training and testing datasets. Later, this mapping relationship is used to recognize the gait in cross-view environment. The problem with these techniques is that they need to construct multiple VTMs to learn the mappings between different view-pairs (*i.e.*, one mapping for each view-pair). In order to cope these limitations, this dissertation propose a novel cross-view gait recognition technique which learns a single model to map the gait sequences from multiple viewpoints to a single canonical view, using a deep neural network. Furthermore, it neither requires the temporally synchronized gait images from multiple cameras nor the information of viewpoint at training and testing time. The cross-view gait descriptors have shown promising results in the desired scenarios.

- **Body Parts Movement Analysis:** A complete framework to analyze the detailed movements of human body parts is proposed. Most existing techniques either use wearable sensors [PLC05; Hei+10] such as inertial measurement unit (IMU) or exploit markers *e.g.* optical [Bur+08; Mei+06] and infrared-based [Rad+09] markers on the human body region to detect and track the body parts with the help of visual sensor. Since such a techniques use multiple sensors/markers on the human body, besides the financial aspects they require their cumbersome installation and calibration. Conversely, the proposed technique does not use any wearable sensors or markers. The proposed framework automatically detects and tracks several body parts in a video sequence, separately. The movements are defined using angle orientations at different joints across the successive frames. The proposed algorithm has been used to build an automatic method to help the clinicians and general practitioners for the early detection of movement disorders in infants. Furthermore, wearing multiple sensors/markers on the infant's body may cause discomfort to them, affecting their natural movements.

- **Body Parts Movement Representation:** An automatic analysis of human movements is momentous in the physiotherapy process to monitor its effects and reactions on the human body. The existing computer-based techniques at rehabilitation and clinical assessment places exploit the skeleton tracking of patient either using the integrated functionality of Microsoft Kinect [LO+13; YXL14] or employ a set of motion sensors [Wan+15; ZTB16] to monitor the movements of the patient during therapy. Although the integrated skeleton tracking of Kinect has triggered a lot of research on human motion analysis at clinical assessment, its limitations that the size of a subject for being integrated body-tracking should be greater than 1 meter and in up-right position in front of the camera, prevent the automatic detection and movement analysis of infants. A framework is introduced to evaluate these movements using the Red-Green-Blue and Depth (RGBD) data. Two novel techniques are proposed to automatically detect the patient body region in the video which is used to construct a multi-dimensional feature vector to represent and analyze these movement patterns

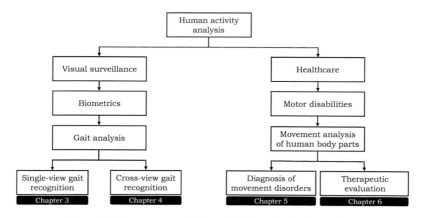

Figure 1.6: An arrangement of contributions in the dissertation.

during therapy. The proposed algorithms have been used to design an effective solution for therapy monitoring and analysis.

1.3 Overview

The rest of the dissertation is organized into six chapters. **Chapter 2** briefly reviews the literature related to the research presented in this dissertation. This is important to understand the existing classical approaches and novelty of the proposed work. The first part of the dissertation consisting of **Chapter 3** and **Chapter 4** presents the contributions in gait recognition. The second part of the dissertation which comprises **Chapter 5** and **Chapter 6**, describes the contributions in the movement analysis of human body parts, as depicted in Figure 1.6. Each proposed technique is evaluated on benchmark datasets and their results are also compared with the existing state-of-the-art in the respective chapters. A brief overview of each chapter is given in the following:

Chapter 2 provides a detailed survey of the existing techniques on gait recognition and the movement analysis of human body parts. Based on the similarities in implementation, the exiting techniques are grouped and their strengths and limitations are presented. A comprehensive overview of the publicly available benchmark gait databases is also presented.

Chapter 3 introduces a novel gait representation and its application in a single-view gait recognition. An evaluation of various motion descriptors is carried out to define the gait representation and their results are discussed.

Chapter 4 presents a cross-view gait recognition technique using a deep fully-connected neural network. First, a gait representation is obtained from the video sequences of an individual's walk using the algorithm described in **Chapter 3**. Later, the view dependent gait representation is transformed into a view invariant gait descriptor using the trained deep network.

Chapter 5 outlines the implementation of a method to help the clinicians in the early detection of movement disorders in infants. The detailed description of the implementation and the proposed model to automatically detect and track the individual's body parts in video is provided.

Chapter 6 describes a computer vision-based system to evaluate the therapeutic procedure. Two novel segmentation techniques are proposed to extract the patient's body region from the RGBD data. The movement patterns in different body parts are encoded in a multi-dimensional feature vector which is classified using machine learning algorithm to classify the accurate movements during therapy.

Chapter 7 concludes this dissertation with a summary of the research and possible directions for future work.

Chapter 2

Related Work

This chapter comprises a literature review of relevant work and describes it based on its similarity to the presented methods. Section 2.1 explains the terminologies used in this dissertation. Section 2.2 surveys the related approaches for gait representation. Subsequently, a summary of the most related methods in cross-view gait recognition is presented in Section 2.3. An overview of publicly available benchmark gait databases, which are evaluated by most of the research community is outlined in Section 2.4. Finally, the approaches relevant to movement analysis of human body parts in the clinical assessment and the rehabilitation process are described in Section 2.5.

2.1 Terminology

For a better understanding of the contents, this section presents a couple of terminologies which are used in the dissertation.

Gait cycle: Gait cycle presents the depiction of movements, which happen during the walk when one foot makes contact with the ground and ends when that same foot contacts the ground again, as shown in Figure 2.1. It consist of two periods namely; stance (when the foot is touching the ground) and swing (limbs are moving through the air).

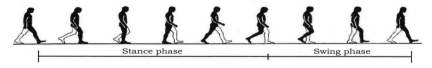

Figure 2.1: Example of a complete gait cycle [Fis+13].

Gait sequence: Gait sequence is the collection of one or more gait cycle(s).

Gait descriptor/signature/representation: Gait descriptor is a feature vector, which is computed from the gait sequence. It can be considered as the representation of gait sequence.

Gallery and probe gait sequences: The gait sequences which are pre-enrolled either in database or used to train a machine learning algorithm are known as gallery, whereas the gait sequences which needs to be recognized are known as probe.

2.2   Gait Representation

The existing gait recognition approaches can be grouped into two broad categories: model-based and appearance-based approaches. The model-based gait recognition approaches employs the human body structure and motion models to identify the individuals. They track different body parts and joint positions over time using the underlying mathematical structure [KFG17]. The structural models [BN07; YNC02; CNC03; Wan+04; BJ01] which may include stick figure, interlinked pendulum and ellipse fitting techniques are generally constructed based on the prior knowledge of the human body shape. The motion models [LG02; Siv+11a; Cha+06; LPV08] use motion information of body parts like joint angle trajectories, rotation patterns of hip and thigh, *etc.*

The appearance-based gait recognition approaches do not use any structural or human motion models. They generally utilize the segmented human body region (known as *silhouette*) directly from the images or video and drive various pieces of information for gait representation, *e.g.* construct a template image from silhouettes images [HB06; Wan+12], extract various gait parameters [ZWY14; GCN08], perform shape analysis [Wan+03a; Kus+11a], and apply various projections [Tan+07c; Tan+07d] on segmented silhouettes. Few approaches have also used the temporal information of human motion [CT12; Kus14] to recognize the individual's gait. Figure 2.2 depicts the distribution of existing gait recognition techniques based upon their underlying model and a short description of few techniques in each category is given in the following sub-sections.

2.2.1   Model-based Approaches

Model-based gait recognition approaches aim to build a gait representation using the human body structure and motion models. In the following, existing pieces of work using both models are introduced.

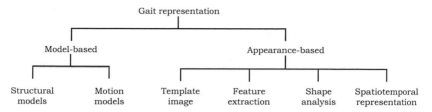

Figure 2.2: The distribution of existing gait recognition techniques into various categories.

Structural models: The structural model defines the structure of different body parts *e.g.* torso, upper and lower limbs, *etc.* by computing some measurements on these regions such as height and width. Usually, these models are built on the prior knowledge of human body shape using stick figure, interlinked pendulum and ellipse fitting techniques. For example, Lee et al. [LG02] proposed the modeling of human body structure using seven different ellipses representing the various body regions. They computed several statistical measurements on these regions over time such as mean, standard deviation, location of its centroid, magnitude and phase of these moment based regions to construct a gait descriptor. The authors in [Cha+06] split the structure of human body region into three parts and the variance of these parts over time are combined to obtain a gait representation. Sivapalan et al. [Siv+11a] proposed a 3D voxel model derived from silhouette images. They construct a voxel model using ellipsoids fitting techniques into four different components of lower limbs. The features derived from the ellipsoids are modeled using a Fourier representation. The authors in [BJ01] computed the distance between different body parts of an individual over time to construct a gait signature.

Motion models: The motion model emphasizes the motion information of human body or its different parts over the time. Yam et al. [YNC02] employed the temporal template matching technique on the gait cycle to extract the angles of thigh and lower leg rotation. They constructed a gait signature using the phase-weighted magnitude of the lower order Fourier components of these rotations. The authors in [CNC03] proposed a motion model using the velocity Hough transform to extract the angular motion of the hip and thigh. Bouchrika et al. [BN07] proposed a motion model using the elliptic Fourier descriptors to extract features from human joints and incorporated them for person identification. The technique proposed in [Wan+04] constructed a structural-based and motion-based model using a condensation framework to refine the feature extraction for gait recognition. The human body structure is modeled using fourteen rigid parts connected to each other at joint locations and the angle trajectories are computed on these locations to construct a gait representation.

Recent studies [YTL14; AN12] have shown that model-based approaches can deal with the occlusion and rotation problems to some extent but are highly dependent on the localization of the torso, and therefore require high-resolution images. They are computationally expensive and sensitive to the quality of video sequences [YTL14].

2.2.2   Appearance-based Approaches

Appearance-based gait recognition approaches operate on the sequence of gait images directly. Usually, they extract human binary silhouettes from the images or video and drive various information for gait representation. Based on similarity in the implementation, the appearance-based approaches can be distributed into following groups.

Template image: The approaches belonging to this family extract the human binary silhouettes from the images and combine them over a gait cycle to obtain a template image, which can be used to identify an individual. Among them, gait energy image (GEI) [HB06] has been extensively used due to its simplicity in implementation and effectiveness. This representation can be obtained by segmenting the human body silhouettes from images through background modeling and averaged them over a gait cycle. However, it loses temporal information in a gait sequence, which is critical to the performance of gait recognition [Wan+12]. Several improvements in GEI, such as frame difference energy image (FDEI) [Che+09], gait entropy image (GEnI) [BXG10b], active energy image (AEI) [ZZX10], chrono-gait image (CGI) [Wan+12], head-torso-thigh image (HTI) [Tan+06], and gait energy volume (GEV) [Siv+11b] have also been proposed. For example, instead of using silhouette images directly, the authors in [Wan+12] used their corresponding contours in a gait cycle and claimed that their proposed representation can preserve the temporal information.

The authors in [HBR12] extract the silhouette shape from the depth images of a walking person and proposed a gait descriptor known as depth gradient histogram energy image (DGHEI). They employed the histogram binning to capture the edges and depth gradient of the person's silhouette from depth images to recognize an individual. The technique proposed in [WBR14] constructed a skeleton based descriptor from a gait cycle known as skeleton variance image (SVIM). They computed skeleton information from the silhouette images using the screened Poisson equation and combining it with motion information proposed a new gait representation. The authors in [LCL11] compute the optical flow fields on extracted silhouettes and formulate a gait representation known as gait flow image (GFI). The technique proposed in [YTL14] computed the Histogram of Optical Flow (HOF) using the silhouette images and averaged them on a gait cycle. This gait representation is known as flow histogram energy image (FHEI).

Feature extraction: The approaches in this category compute various gait related parameters from the human body silhouettes over time, *e.g.* height and width ratio, silhouette area, width and centroid of the contour, and used them to recognize an individual. For example, the technique proposed in [GCN08] extracts the height and width features from the normalized and scaled silhouette region to construct a gait representation. In [ZWY14], the authors computed the height and width ratio and centroid of the contour, and used them to approximate the individual's gait through RBF network and deterministic learning. Tan et al. [Tan+07b] build a normalized pseudo-height and width (NPHW) histogram on the sequence of segmented silhouettes, to recognize an individual. Moreover, they used relevant component analysis (RCA) to improve data separability in gait recognition. The authors in [Siv+13] proposed the fusion of Histogram of Oriented Gradient (HOG) and local directional patterns (LDP) to obtain a gait representation. The techniques proposed in [Tan+07c; Tan+07d; Tan+07a] employed the normalized segmented silhouette's region and projected them in different directions such as horizontal and diagonal. They computed a vector of projective values in each projection and used them to identify the walker.

Shape analysis: The techniques in this category exploit the shape analysis of segmented silhouettes over time to obtain a gait representation. For example, the authors in [Wan+03b] proposed the mapping of 2D silhouette into one dimensional (1D) normalized distance signal by contour unwrapping. The variations in the shape of 1D silhouette over time are used to approximate the gait patterns. Dadashi et al. [DASZ09] proposed a gait representation from silhouette images using wavelet packet library. They computed the 1D representation of silhouette using [Wan+03b] and analyzed them through wavelet packet transform to construct a gait representation. The authors in [Wan+03a] employed Procrustes Shape Analysis (PSA) to obtain procrustes mean shape (PMS) from a sequence of silhouette's contour as gait descriptor. The authors claim that PMS represents both the motion and body shape into a unified descriptor. Several improvements in [Wan+03a] such as, pairwise shape configuration (PSC) [Kus+11a], higher-order derivative shape configuration (HSC) [Kus+11b], differential composition model (DCM) [Kus+12b] and gait curves [DR10] have been also been proposed. For example, Kusakunniran et al. [Kus+11a] proposed an improved version of PSA with the addition of local shape information and precise boundary segmentation. The authors in [DR10] proposed the computation of gait curves using few static features (*e.g.* height, centroid, *etc.*) from binary silhouette and

PSA is used to recognize an individual. The technique proposed in [BCD04] employed the concept of self similarity plot (SSP) to encode the projection of gait dynamics and hence a 2D signature of gait.   Specifically, SSP comprises a matrix of cross-correlation between each pair of silhouettes in the sequence, which is used to construct a gait feature. During the identification, the similarity with the largest probability recognises an individual.

Spatiotemporal representation: The approaches belonging to this category use motion information of a walking person to construct a gait representation. For example, the technique proposed in [Cas+16] computed the spatiotemporal cuboids of optical flow from the video sequences and fed to Convolutional Neural Network (CNN) to obtain a high level gait representation. The technique proposed in [Kus14] extracts spatiotemporal interest points from the video sequence and constructs a high level gait representation based on it, namely, histogram of space-time interest points descriptors (HSD). Choudhury et al. [CT12] employed the spatiotemporal motion characteristics, and statistical and physical parameters (STM–SPP) such as height and width of silhouette's contour in a gait cycle, to construct a gait descriptor. The method proposed in [Bas+09] captured the motion intensity and its direction information using optical flow field, and formulated a histogram based gait representation. The authors in [LB98] computed the shape of motion from optical flow field in a gait sequence to generate a feature vector for individual recognition. Hu et al. [Hu+13a] employed local binary patterns (LBP) to describe the texture information in optical flow and used them to recognise an individual.

In comparison with model-based approaches, the appearance-based approaches are capable to recognize the individuals even from the relatively low-resolution images and they are computationally efficient too [YTL14; ZWY14]. They have demonstrated promising recognition results on various benchmark gait databases. However, their recognition accuracy is highly dependent on the precise segmentation of silhouette from the background which is still a challenging problem in the literature. An inaccurate segmentation of silhouette shape may disrupt the construction of gait descriptor and degrade the recognition accuracy [ZWY14].

2.3   Cross-view Gait Recognition

The variation in the appearance of a person's walk due to change in viewing angle is the most challenging and unavoidable problem in practical surveillance systems since the CCTVs are usually installed in public places at different positions and altitudes, and a person can change his/her walking direction too, based on his/her destination. Consequently, the change in viewing angle significantly alters the gait representation to measure their similarity. It introduces intra-personal variations which is always larger than inter-personal variations caused by other covariates factors such as clothing, walking surface and *etc*. Thus, the 2D gait representation from different viewpoints must be normalized before their similarity is measured [Wu+17]. To cope with this problem, numerous techniques have been proposed and they can be distributed into three categories: view-invariant gait descriptors [PP+16; Zha+17], construction of 3D gait descriptors [Bod+09; Zha+06], and view-transformation model based representation [Wu+17; YZC15]. The first family of techniques develop a view-invariant gait descriptor by transforming the sample of gait sequences from different viewpoints to a common subspace. The approaches belonging to second category construct a 3D gait descriptor using multiple calibrated cameras, whereas the approaches in the third category learn a mapping between the gait sequences perceived from multiple viewpoints. In the following, some recent pieces of work in each category are presented.

2.3.1 View-invariant Gait Descriptor

The approaches in this category construct a view-invariant gait descriptor by transforming/projecting the gait features from different viewpoints into a common discriminative subspace, where the similarity measurement is carried out. Specifically, the objective is to learn a discriminative projection in such a way that it maximizes the relevances of instances of the same person from distinct views while minimizing the relevance of instances of different persons in the projection subspace [Zha+17]. These approaches can be further classified into geometry-based [KCC03; JBA09], subspace learning-based [PP+16; LLT11] and metric learning-based [Mur+12] approaches. The geometry based approaches employ the geometrical properties of an individual in the gait sequences. For example, the technique proposed in [KCC03] used the perspective projection model to obtain a side-view gait images of an individual from any arbitrary viewpoint by assuming that a walking person is a 2D planar object in the sagittal plane. The authors in [JBA09] proposed the transformation of motion trajectories from any arbitrary view to a standard plane and their similarities are compared to recognize an individual.

The subspace learning-based approaches learn a joint subspace using the gait descriptors from training data. The view-invariant features for testing sequences are obtained by projecting them on the learned subspace. The authors in [Zha+17] proposed discriminative projection with list-wise constraints and rectification (DPLCR) to learn a projection, which can map the gait features from different views to a common discriminative subspace. Specifically, they build a similarity list for each subject with the rest and the list is obtained after the discriminative projection is enforced to be as close as to the predefined one. The authors in [PP+16] employ subspace learning using direct linear discriminant analysis (DLDA) to create a single projection model for classification. The technique proposed in [LLT11] learns a joint subspace of gait features using joint principal component analysis (JPCA), to pair them with different view angles. The authors in [BXG10a; Kus+14] used the canonical correlation analysis (CCA) to project each pair of gait sequence into two subspaces with maximal correlation. However, these techniques construct multiple mapping matrices, *i.e.*, one for each pair of viewpoints. The technique proposed in [Hu14] employed a sparse local discriminant CCA to model the correlation of gait features from different views. They used the correlation strength as similarity measure. Metric learning based approaches compute a weighting vector comprising the similarity score related to each feature, which is used to estimate the recognition score. The technique proposed in [Mur+12] learns the transformation matrices using a 3D gait model of multiple subjects. They employed these matrices to transform the gait features from different views in gallery to the features with the same view as the probe. The authors in [MFX12] proposed the use of pairwise RankSVM algorithm [CK10] to improve the gait recognition with several variations, such as, view, clothing and carrying.

These approaches perform quite well for specific scenarios, particularly when the view change is not large enough. Usually, they are hard to generalize for other cases and their feature extraction phase is also disrupted due to self occlusion [Wu+17].

2.3.2   3D View Gait Descriptor

The approaches belonging to this category assume that the temporally synchronized images of a walking subject are available from multiple cameras. They construct a 3D gait descriptor using multi-view synchronized images. For example, the authors in [Bod+09] proposed a 3D visual hull model to construct a view-invariant gait descriptor using the input images from multiple cameras. Ariyanto et al. [AN12] introduced a 3D gait recognition approach using a marionette and mass-spring model with 3D voxel gait data. The articulation in the human body is modeled using a stick-figure which emulates the marionettes' motion and joint structure. The 11 nodes of stick-figure describe the joint locations such as head, torso, and lower legs. The technique proposed in [LF+16] computes the 3D angular data of the subject's movement to construct a view-invariant gait descriptor. The authors in [ZT05] proposed a 3D linear model to construct a view-independent gait descriptor using Bayesian rules. Zhao et al. [Zha+06] constructed a 3D human model for gait recognition using the video sequences captured from multiple viewpoints. They used motion trajectories of the limbs and the length of body segments, to recognise the 3D gait. The authors in [Tan+17] constructed a 3D parametric model using pose and shape deformation from a template model of 2D silhouette images. The view-invariant gait recognition is carried out using partial similarity matching.

These techniques require costly setup of multiple calibrated cameras, expensive computation and can only be used in a controlled environment; therefore, they are not suitable for real world applications [PP+16]. The authors in [NMY13; Kas+16] used the Microsoft Kinect sensor along with its tracking functionality to construct the 3D gait representation. They employed the skeleton information of a walking person to recognize him/her. However, the use of such 3D sensors suffer with the limitation of sensor's range and its unreliable estimation in darkness and infrared absorbing objects.

2.3.3   View Transformation Model

View Transformation Model (VTM) based approaches learn a mapping/transformation relationship among the gait features, perceived from different viewpoints. Lately, the learned relationship is used to construct the cross-view gait descriptors prior to measure their similarity. Such approaches can deal with view variations without relying on multiple cameras or camera calibration.

Makihara et al. [Mak+06] proposed a singular value decomposition (SVD) based VTM to project frequency-domain based features from one view to another. The authors in [Kus+09b] employed linear discriminant analysis (LDA) to optimize the gait features and train a VTM for each of the two views. Instead of using the SVD, the technique proposed in [Kus+10] computes the local motion gait features and build a VTM using support vector regression (SVR). The authors in [Hu13] proposed a gait descriptor namely enhanced Gabor gait (EGG), which employs a non-linear mapping to encode the statistical and structural characteristics of gait across the views. They exploit regularized local tensor discriminant analysis (RLTDA) to capture the nonlinear manifolds. The technique presented in [Hu+13b] used a unitary linear projection to construct a cross-view gait descriptor. The authors in [Wu+17; Shi+16] proposed to learn a deep CNN using the GEI to measure the similarity between the gait representation of different views. Yan et al. [YZC15] employ GEI with CNN to predict multiple attributes for cross-view gait recognition. In comparison with the aforementioned two categories, the VTM based techniques have demonstrated excellent recognition accuracy and can be directly applied to the viewpoints which are significantly different from the side view, *e.g.* frontal or back view [Wu+17]. However, the majority of existing methods in this category, such as [Wu+17; YZC15], used segmented silhouette of a walking subject to construct a gait feature, *e.g.* GEI, and build a VTM to transform the gait features from one view to another view. Few other methods [BXG10a; Kus+14] construct multiple mapping matrices, one for each pair of viewpoints.

These techniques are applicable to solve both cross-view and multi-view gait recognition problems, and do not require multiple calibrated cameras. Moreover, they are computationally efficient and thus, suitable for real-time applications [Kus+12a].

2.4 Benchmark Gait Databases

Gait recognition has gained the interest of the research community from the early nineties, and some algorithm were also proposed to identify a person using gait. Since no benchmark gait database was available at that time, they suffered to evaluate their methods on realistic walking scenarios. The first gait database was developed in 2001 with 33 subjects and later it was extended to more than 100 subjects [Sar+05]. Following this, a number of gait databases were developed with different covariates. The rest of this section introduces the available benchmark gait databases.

CASIA Gait Databases

The CASIA (Chinese Academy of Sciences Institute of Automation) gait database consists of four datasets: CASIA-A, CASIA-B, CASIA-C and CASIA-D. A short description of each of the datasets is given in the following:

CASIA-A: CASIA-A [Wan+03b] contains the walk sequences of 20 subjects recorded in an outdoor environment. Every subject in the database has four walk sequences, recorded from three different viewing angles: 0° (*i.e.*, lateral view), 45° (i.e., oblique view) and 90° (*i.e.*, frontal view). Each subject walks twice, from left-to-right and from right-to-left.

CASIA-B: CASIA-B [Yu+06] is a large database comprising the walk sequences of 124 subjects, recorded from 11 different viewing angles. The videos are captured in a well controlled labortorical environment at 25 frames-per-second (f/s) with three different variations in walking style, namely: normal walk, walk with bag and walk with coat. There are ten walking sequences for each subject: six sequences of normal walk, two sequences of walk while carrying the bag and two sequences of walk while wearing a coat.

CASIA-C: CASIA-C [Tan+06] comprises the gait sequences of 153 subjects with four walking scenarios: normal walk, slow walk, fast walk, and walk with backpack. The video sequences are captured at night using a low resolution thermal camera at 25 f/s. Each subject in the database has four sequences of normal walk and two sequences for the rest of each.

CASIA-D: CASIA-D [Zhe+12] consists of the walk sequences of 88 subjects. The recording was held in an indoor environment and the foot pressure images of walkers were also saved.

CMU MoBo Gait Database

The CMU MoBo (The Carnegie Mellon University Motion of Body) [GS01] database contains the gait sequences of 25 subjects while walking on a treadmill. The recording was held in an indoor environment at 30 f/s. Each subject has four walk scenarios: slow walk, fast walk, slow walk with ball in hands, and slow walk at certain slope. The database was recorded using 6 cameras distributed evenly around the treadmill to capture the sequences with different viewing angles.

TUM GAID Gait Database

TUM GAID (Technical University of Munich gait audio image and depth) [HBR12] is also another large gait database, comprising 3,370 walk sequences of 305 subjects. The database was recorded in two different seasons in an outdoor environment, using a Microsoft Kinect camera. During the first recording, a total of 176 subjects' walk sequences are captured, whereas the second recording contains the walk sequences of 161 subjects. A subset of 32 subjects participated in both recordings, therefore the database contains the walk sequences of 305 individuals. Ten walk sequences are captured for each subject, namely normal walk, walk with backpack and walk with coating shoes. Each subject has six sequences of normal walk, two sequences for each of the rest, recorded from left-to-right and from right-to-left walk. The subjects in the subset of 32 people who participated in both recordings, have ten walk sequences in each recording session (*i.e.*, 20 sequences in total).

OU-ISIR Gait Databases

Recently, the Institute of Scientific and Industrial Research (ISIR), Osaka University (OU) has provided several gait datasets with different variations. The short description of a few of them is explained in the following.

OU-Treadmill: The OU-ISIR treadmill dataset [Mak+12] contains the gait sequences of subjects while they are walking on a treadmill. The recording was held in an indoor environment at 60 f/s. The dataset has three further parts: The first part (named as treadmill dataset A) comprises the walk sequences of 34 subjects with variations in speed. The second part (known as treadmill dataset B) contains the gait sequences of 68 subjects with variations in clothing. The third part (named as treadmill dataset D) comprises the sequences of 185 subjects with fluctuations among periods. Each subject has two sequences of gallery and probe.

OULP: The OU-ISIR large population (OULP) [Iwa+12] is a large cross-view gait database which comprises the gait sequences of more than 4,000 subjects. The gait sequences are recorded in a well controlled indoor environment at 30 f/s, under four viewing angles: $55°$, $65°$, $75°$ and $85°$. Each subject was asked to walk along a course in a natural manner. There are 3 walk sequences for each subject.

GaitST: The OU-ISIR gait speed transition dataset (GaitST) [Man+14b] was captured in an indoor environment and consists of two parts. Part one comprises the recognizable gait sequences of 26 subjects walking on a floor and part two contains the recognizable gait sequences of 25 subjects walking on a treadmill. Furthermore, the gallery set in both parts consists of 178 and 179 subjects respectively, while the subjects are walking on a treadmill.

OU-MVLP: In very recent times, the OU-ISIR has distributed the biggest multi-view large population dataset (MVLP) so far, which contains the gait sequences of $10,307$ subjects. The dataset was recorded in an indoor environment, under 14 viewing angles and the subjects have repeated a forward and backward walk twice.

SOTON

University of Southampton human identification at a distance (SOTON) [Dd05] database is captured in both indoor and outdoor environments, and consists of two parts. The first part contains the gait sequences of 100 subjects with variations in viewing angle. The data is recorded when the subjects were walking in frontal and lateral view. The second part comprises the sequences of 10 subjects with variations in footwear, clothing and carrying bags during the walk.

USF HumanID Gait Baseline database

USF (University of South Florida) gait database [Sar+05] comprises $1,870$ walk sequences from 122 subjects. The dataset is recorded in an outdoor environment with the variations of viewing angle, footwear, carrying condition and clothing.

Table 2.1: Summary of existing gait databases, which are grouped with respect to their provided agencies. The terms *cl, bg, ft, sp* and *cr* represent the variations in *clothing, bag, footwear, speed* and *carrying objects*, respectively during the walk. Views represents the number of viewing angles which are used in the database recording, − represents that no variations in the gait sequences are recorded, and * is denoting the databases which have been used by most of the research community in their recent proposed techniques.

Database	Subjects	Views	Covariates	Environment	Walking surface	Year
CASIA-A	20	3	−	outdoor	floor	2001
CASIA-B *	124	11	*cl, bg*	indoor	floor	2005
CASIA-C *	153	1	*cl, bg, sp*	outdoor	floor	2005
CASIA-D	88	1	−	indoor	floor/pressure mat	2009
CMU MoBo *	25	6	*bg, sp, cr*	indoor	treadmill	2001
TUM GAID *	305	1	*bg, ft*	outdoor	floor	2012
OU-Treadmill-A	34	1	*sp*	indoor	treadmill	2012
OU-Treadmill-B	68	1	*cl*	indoor	treadmill	2012
OU-Treadmill-D	185	1	*sp*	indoor	treadmill	2012
OULP *	4,016	4	−	indoor	floor	2012
GaitST-1	178	1	*sp*	indoor	floor/treadmill	2014
GaitST-2	179	1	−	indoor	treadmill	2014
OU-MVLP	10,307	14	−	indoor	floor	2018
SOTON-1	100	2	−	both	floor	2002
SOTON-2	12	4	*ft, cl, cr*	indoor	floor	2002
USF *	122	2	*ft, cl, cr*	outdoor	treadmill	2001
AVAMVG	20	6	−	indoor	floor	2013
KY 4D	42	16	−	indoor	floor	2010
UMD-1	25	1	−	outdoor	floor	2001
UMD-2	55	2	−	outdoor	floor	2001
UMD-3	12	5	−	outdoor	floor	2001
GTD	20	3	−	both	floor	2001
KinectREID	71	3	*bg, cr*	indoor	floor	2016

Others

Some other gait databases, such as Kinect based person re-identification dataset (Kinec-tREID) [Pal+16], Georgia Tech. (Georgia Institute of Technology) database (GTD) [oCo01], University of Maryland database (UMD), [HU01], Kyushu University 4D gait database (KY 4D) [Iwa+10] and the AVA (Applications of Artificial Vision) multi-view dataset for gait recognition (AVAMVG) [LF+14] have been collected and distributed to the community to evaluate their algorithms for person identification using gait. The short description of all databases is summarized in Table 2.1.

2.5   Movement Analysis

The movement analysis of different body parts of humans plays an important role in better clinical and behavioral assessment, and more efficient therapeutic decision making accordingly. This section presents the summary of automated and semi-automated techniques to support physiotherapy and rehabilitation processes to restore the functional ability of the patients. Over the last years, numerous computer-based techniques have been proposed to assess the human's motion information and perform quantitative analysis. Based on the sensors being used in capturing the motion information, they can be distributed in two groups: vision-based and sensor-based [Kha+18c]. The first family of techniques used either markers on human body region and tracked them in the successive frames of a video or exploits markerless solutions to detect and track different body parts using image features such as colour, edges, *etc*. The second group of techniques employ motion sensors such as IMU to capture the motion information. Figure 2.3 depicts the distribution of existing techniques to analyze the movements of human body parts based upon the source device and underlying model. The short description of few techniques in each category is described in the following two sub-sections.

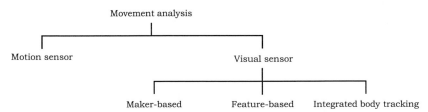

Figure 2.3: The distribution of existing techniques for movement analysis into various categories.

2.5.1 Visual Sensor-based Approaches

The set of techniques in this category either used contrast images or depth images and can be further classified into three subgroups. First group of techniques employ markers on the human body region to represent the joint locations, and used them to detect and track skeletal information in a video. The markers information in the image is used to identify the position and orientation of joints. The second group of techniques do not use any markers on human body region and detect the joints information using the image features such as colour, shape, edges, *etc.* Similar to the second one, the third group of techniques also do not use any markers and track the joint locations using the integrated body tracking functionality of visual sensors.

Marker-based techniques: Marker-based techniques capture the motion information based on the tracking of markers (*e.g.* reflective spheres, gloves with light-emitting diodes, or infrared markers) in the successive frames of a video. For example, the authors in [Bur+08] proposed two games for upper limb stroke rehabilitation, which are controlled by colour object segmentation and its tracking for motion detection. The colour objects are attached to the upper limbs and the algorithm detects them using calibration process and tracks them in successive frames. Similarly, the authors in [TH04] proposed a colour marker based tracking algorithm to detect the motion information at different joints. They attached different colour markers on joint locations and then tracked in successive frames of a video. Moreover, the tracking results are compared with the results obtained from commercial infrared marker based tracking system. The authors in [Che+17a] proposed a therapy system for upper limbs movement using an infrared camera with hand skateboard training device. Patients participating in the therapy have a binding band attached to a hand skateboard on the table to guide the patient in moving the hand skateboard along the designated path to train the patient's upper limbs. Meinecke et al. [Mei+06] proposed a motion analysis system using seven visual cameras to capture the motion of 3D markers, attached to the infant's body region. They used the motion information of markers in predicting the risk for developing movement disorders. The authors in [Rad+09] introduced an unsupervised patient rehabilitation method with the help of marker based motion tracking of knee movements using infrared optical tracker. They detect the errors in movement and demonstrated to the user how to perform the movement correctly. The authors in [Led+08] proposed a 3D position sensing device to measure human motion using a tiny high resolution video camera and a fixed IR emitting target. The authors in [Pao+14] proposed a system for the tracking of foot positioning and orientation for gait training. The foot is detected and tracked using colour markers.

The use of such marker sensors requires extra equipments. Besides the financial aspects, they require to attach many markers on the human body and cumbersome installation and calibration. The colour based markers suffer from the reduction of tracking efficiency due the high incidence of motion blurs [DG+12].

Feature-based techniques: Instead of using markers on human body, the markerless motion capturing systems exploit the image features such as shape colour, edges, pixel's location to detect and track the different body parts. The research in this domain has received a lot of attention in recent years, particularly since the availability of inexpensive 3D sensors, such as Microsoft Kinect. For example, Shotton et al. [Sho+13] proposed a method to predict the 3D positions of body joints in depth image. They employed the depth comparison features for each pixel and classified into human body parts using random forest classifier. The improved version of [Sho+13] is proposed by Hesse et al. [Hes+15]. They exploited pixel-wise body part classification in depth data using random ferns to estimate the infant's body pose. The information of angle orientation at predicted joints is used for motion analysis. The technique proposed in [Ols+14] applied the body part model fitting technique comprising of basic shape on depth images to segment the infant's body region and capture their movements in successive frames. The authors in [PD13] proposed a model fitting technique into depth images of Kinect sensor, targeting rehabilitation exercises during physiotherapy. They captured the motion of human leg by fitting a model and optimization is performed by particle filtering. The authors in [Sta+12; Rah+14] used optical flow, computed from infant's limbs to analyze the movement patterns. However, they suffer with the localization of movements at particular joint. The technique proposed in [Eve+11] introduced a game for stroke rehabilitation, using the movements and gestures of hands. They used two cameras, an optical camera and a thermal camera, to recognize hand gestures. However, the proposed methodology is limited to recognize only two gestures (hand open and closed).

Integrated body tracking functionality: In recent years, with the invention of a very low cost device, *i.e.*, Microsoft Kinect, a new tool is now to be considered in rehabilitation, as well as in assessment, which provides a markerless motion capturing system. It provides Red-Green-Blue (RGB) image and the depth information of the captured scene, which facilitate to create a 3D view of the environment. Moreover, an important feature of the depth sensors is skeleton tracking, which has been utilized by the several researchers at ambient assisted living and rehabilitation places. For example, the authors in [Wu11] calculated the 3D coordinates distances between 15 joints using the integrated human skeleton from Kinect, and used them to monitor the rehabilitation progress. The authors in [LO+13; Aco12] proposed rehabilitation systems using the integrated skeleton tracking of Kinect and the study of 11 subjects in their research have shown the significant improvements in the standard motor assessments. The technique proposed in [GUQ13] extracts the patient's posture information from the Kinect and compares it with a model posture, which is required in some exercises to strengthen the body muscles. Yao et al. [YXL14] employs the integrated skeleton information of Kinect, and proposed a system to compare and evaluate the patients' movement by providing them a feedback on the screen. The technique proposed in [Cha+12] employs the integrated motion tracking of upper limbs using Kinect for rehabilitation. They also validate the results of Kinect sensor using the outputs of OptiTrack[1]. The authors in [CCH11] used the motion tracking information from Kinect and proposed a rehabilitation system to assist the therapists in their work. The system is designed for children suffering from motor disabilities and presents the rehabilitation progress to the therapists, as per defined standards. Research in [Exe+13] used Kinect's skeletal tracking to analyze the rehabilitation in upper limbs. Recent surveys on various therapy techniques for rehabilitation using Kinect can be found in [DG+15; MHK14].

Although the invention of Kinect sensor has triggered a lot of research on human motion analysis, rehabilitation and clinical assessment, its limitation that the size of a subject for being integrated body-tracking should be greater than 1 meter, prevent the automatic detection and movement analysis of infants. Moreover, it also requires that the subject should be in up-right position in front of the camera.

2.5.2 Motion Sensor-based Algorithms

Motion sensors which may include accelerometers, gyroscopes, magnetometers have been used in a variety of clinical applications and rehabilitation systems to capture the human motion. For example, the rehabilitation exercise proposed in [Che+15] used tri-axial accelerometers on the chest, thigh and shank of the working leg to assess the rehabilitation progress of a patient suffering with knee osteoarthritis. Hester et al. [Hes+06] proposed a rehabilitation system using four accelerometers, attached on human upper limbs and chest to assess the motor ability of stroke patients. The features are extracted from each time segment for linear regression to predict clinical scores of motor abilities. The authors in [Tse+09] proposed a system using a set of accelerometers and compass to capture human motion for home rehabilitation. The sensors are attached on specified movable body parts and the system will assign a score based on the quality of movement, defined by the therapists. The authors in [PLC05] developed a wireless sensor namely Eco that can be attached to the arms

---

[1]http://optitrack.com/

and legs of a patient having probable movement disorders. Upon movement, the sensors send signals to the Eco-station, which is connected with a monitor screen. The screen will show the motion information in respective limbs. The authors in [Hei+10] captured the movements of infants' limbs using four accelerometers, attached with them. They used decision tree algorithm to classify these movements into healthy and abnormal. The authors in [Bry+06] used electrogoniometer (an electric device to measure the angles at joints) to capture the motion information at different joints of children suffering from CP during the exercise. They employed such a motion information in a virtual reality (VR) based game and claim that patients have shown great interest, performed more repetitions of the exercise, and generated more ankle dorsiflexion in comparison with standalone exercise. Admittedly, VR based gaming applications offer an interactive, engaging and effective environment for physical therapy; however, they require expensive hardware and software setup. Moreover, they are designed to suit a specific class of patients and could not be useful in case of young patients, since they cannot interact with such systems.

The technique proposed in [ZTB16] used a wireless human motion monitoring system for gait analysis in rehabilitation process. It used a set of IMUs to estimate the joint rotation in three dimensions, and a pair of smart shoes with pressure sensors to measure the force distributions between the two feet during walk. Another similar study is proposed in [Pra+11], which used two accelerometers placed on each leg for gait analysis in stroke survivors. The authors in [Che+11] developed a monitoring system for patients suffering with Parkinson's disease (PD). The system used wireless accelerometers sensors attached with patients body parts and can remotely monitor the patient's movements. The movement information is shared with the clinic using a web-based system. Patel et al. [Pat+09] proposed a system using eight accelerometers attached with upper and lower limbs to assess the severity of motor complications in patients with PD. The authors in [BHP11] proposed the integration of Kalman filtering with inertial sensors to resolve the problems, related to measurement errors and improve the overall estimation of human motion. Manson et al. [Man+00] used a tri-axial accelerometer placed on the shoulder to analyze the severity of dyskinesia's (*i.e.*, side-effect of medication) in patients suffering from PD. They claimed that there is a correlation between the output of accelerometers and the severity of dyskinesia's in patient. Instead of using a set of individual sensors, the authors in [Ble+13] proposed a sensing jacket for home based exercise trainer system to capture the user's motion information, which is compared with the desired exercises. The proposed sensing jacket used ten IMUs to track human movements. Similarly, a smart rehabilitation garment is proposed in [Wan+15] using IMUs to support posture correction. The systems alerts the user by vibrating on the garment and visual instructions on smartphone using Bluetooth connection.

However, the limitation of such techniques is that they require to wear a number of sensors on the human body, which may cause discomfort to them (particularly for young patients) and may affect their natural movements [Kha+16b].

Chapter 3

Single-view Gait Recognition

Recall it is concluded from the literature review (**Chapter 2**) that in contrast to model-based gait recognition approaches, the appearance-based approaches are more effective and efficient [YTL14; ZWY14]. However, the existing appearance-based gait representation frameworks, such as GEI [HB06] is illustrated in Figure 3.1, have various limitations. This representation is proposed by Han et al. [HB06], and has been extensively used in gait applications due to its simple implementation and higher recognition results in specific scenarios. It is computed by segmenting the human body's silhouette from the images using background modeling and averaging them over a gait cycle. The problem with such silhouette based gait recognition techniques is that they require a precise segmentation of human silhouette shape from the images which is still a challenging problem in the literature. An inaccurate segmentation may deteriorate the recognition rate [ZWY14]. Therefore, the gait representation proposed in this chapter primarily belongs to the category of appearance-based approaches, but it is segmentation free and is able to achieve excellent recognition accuracy.

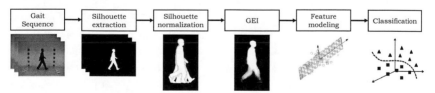

Figure 3.1: An example of silhouette based gait representation framework.

3.1   Gait Recognition using Spatiotemporal Motion Characteristics

This chapter presents a gait recognition framework using the spatiotemporal motion characteristics of an individual's walk. The proposed gait recognition algorithm does not require human body segmentation or the gait-cycle estimation from the gait sequence. The representation can be estimated in four steps. First, the dense trajectories in a video sequence are extracted using the optical flow field, and their motion information is saved in local descriptors. Second, a codebook based on Gaussian mixture model is computed using the motion descriptors from the training dataset. Third, the local descriptors are transformed to high level representation using Fisher vector encoding and earlier computed codebook. Fourth, the encoded vectors are fused through the representation level fusion and classified using simple linear support vector machine. A block diagram representing the entire process is shown in Figure 3.2. The experimental evaluation of the proposed technique is carried out on five large benchmark gait databases and the recognition results are compared with the existing state-of-the-art techniques. The implementation details of each step are described in the subsequent sections.

3.1.1   Motion Descriptors

The low-level local features play an important role in detecting and representing a local region in an image/video. Numerous feature detectors such as 3D-Harris [Lap05], Dense Trajectories [WS13], Cuboid [Dol+05] have been proposed to detect the interested region in this regard. To describe the detected region, several hand-crafted feature descriptors have been proposed and successfully exploited in various computer vision problems; HOG [DT05], HOF [DTS06], Motion Boundary Histogram (MBH) [Wan+13] are a few to mention. Usually, multiple descriptors are fused to efficiently represent the certain aspects of a local region such as static appearance and motion [Kha+17].

Recently, the dense trajectories have demonstrated promising results in recognizing the actions in video data [Pen+16]. The motivation to use them in gait recognition is that they encode the local motion patterns of an individual's walk and they can be computed easily from a video sequence. In order to extract dense trajectories, a set of point is chosen from a frame and is tracked in the successive frames using displacement information from optical flow field. In particular, each point $P_i = (x_i, y_i)$ in frame i is tracked in the frame $i+1$ from a dense optical flow field. The concatenation of these sample points in the subsequent frames (*i.e.*, $P_i, P_{i+1}, P_{i+2}, \ldots$) represent the trajectory. In a given trajectory of length L, a sequence of displacement vector $\mathcal{D}$ can be computed as follows,

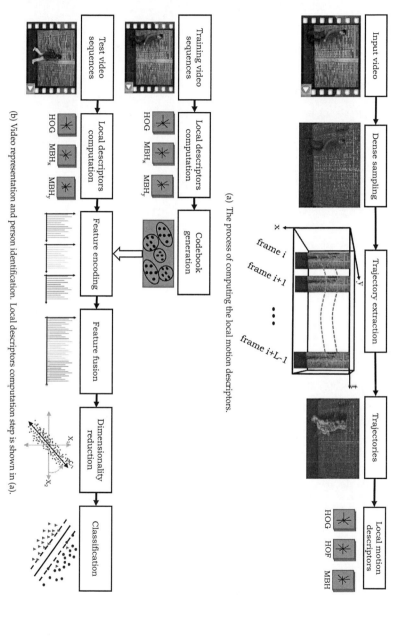

Figure 3.2: Schematic diagram of the proposed spatiotemporal gait representation algorithm for person identification.

$$\mathcal{D} = (\Delta P_i, \Delta P_{i+1}, \ldots, \Delta P_{i+L-1}), \tag{3.1}$$

where

$$\Delta P_i = (P_{i+1} - P_i) = (x_{i+1} - x_i, y_{i+1} - y_i) \tag{3.2}$$

The displacement vector $\mathcal{D}$ is normalized as,

$$S = \frac{(\Delta P_i, \ldots, \Delta P_{i+L-1})}{\sum_{j=i}^{i+L-1} \left\| \Delta P_j \right\|}, \tag{3.3}$$

where S is representing the trajectory descriptor. The authors in [WS13] proposed the computation of HOG and HOF descriptors along the dense trajectories for action recognition. Moreover, the relative motion information between the pixels along horizontal and vertical axes are encoded by computing the derivative along the respective components of the optical flow and their information is kept in two histograms, namely MBH_x (*i.e.*, Motion Boundary Histogram) and MBH_y respectively. The descriptors are computed within a space-time volume of size 32 by 32 pixels and with 15 frames. The volume is subdivided into four blocks to encode the structure information and the size of each block is set to 16 by 16 pixels by 5 frames. The information of each local descriptor is saved using the quantization of their orientation information into 8-bin histogram, and they are normalized with L_2-norm separately. The process for the computation of local motion descriptors is illustrated in Figure 3.2a.

The evaluation of these local descriptors with several combinations is carried out to assess their effectiveness for person identification using gait. Among them, few of the evaluation results on TUM GAID database [HBR12] are shown in Figure 3.3, and it can be observed that the composition of HOG and MBH outperforms the rest. Since HOG contains the information of a person's static appearance and MBH highlights the changes in optical flow field (*i.e.*, motion boundaries), combining both pieces of information has greater impact in identifying a person using his/her appearance and local motion characteristics [KFG17]. Additionally, they are capable of capturing small changes in the gait patterns.

3.1.2   Codebook Generation

Usually, the local descriptors are used to construct a high-level representation of an image or video and this process in known as *feature encoding* [Pen+16; Tie+16]. The local descriptors in the proposed gait recognition algorithm are encoded using Fisher vector (FV) encoding and a codebook based on Gaussian mixture model (GMM). The idea of FV is derived from Fisher

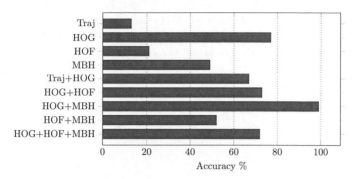

Figure 3.3: Evaluation of several descriptors for gait recognition on TUM GAID database.

kernel [Sán+13] which employs the traits of both discriminative and generic approaches. GMM is a generative model which describes the distribution over feature space and can be expressed as [KFG18a]:

$$p(X \mid \Theta) = \sum_{k=1}^{K} w_k \mathcal{N}(x \mid \mu_k, \Sigma_k), \tag{3.4}$$

where $k = 1, 2, \ldots, K$ is representing the mixture (also known as cluster) number, w_k is the weight of k-th mixture and μ_k, Σ_K are the mean vector and the covariance matrix of the k-th mixture, respectively. Moreover, $\mathcal{N}(x \mid \mu_k, \Sigma_k)$ is representing the D-dimensional Gaussian distribution which can be described as:

$$\mathcal{N}(x \mid \mu_k, \Sigma_k) = \frac{1}{\sqrt{(2\pi)^D |\Sigma_k|}} e^{-\frac{1}{2}(x-\mu_k)^T \Sigma_k^{-1}(x-\mu_k)} \tag{3.5}$$

Moreover, $\Theta = \{w_k, \mu_k, \Sigma_k, k = 1, 2, \ldots, K\}$ in Equation 3.4 is representing the set of model parameters, which seeks its optimal values either using maximum likelihood estimation (MLE) or maximum a posterior probability (MAP) [TK09]. The MLE method's aim is to seek the best values for Θ so that the likelihood function takes its maximum value. The MLE for Θ can be described as:

$$\Theta_{MLE} = \arg\max_{\Theta} \log \prod_t p(x_t \mid \Theta) \tag{3.6}$$

It can be observed from the Equation 3.6 that one need to derive the log-likelihood of the model and maximize it with respect to Θ using some optimization algorithm such as gradient descent (*i.e.*, gradient of the likelihood function with respect to Θ). Since it is convenient to work with the natural logarithm of the likelihood function and it is monotonically increasing too, the maximization of the likelihood function is equivalent to its maximization using the log of the function. Whereas, MAP assumed that Θ is unknown parameter, select its value randomly and maximized over the feature set $X = \{x_t, t = 1, \ldots, T\}$. Since MAP works on a posterior distribution which can be obtained using the product of likelihood and prior probability (*i.e.*, Bayes theorem), and can be written as:

$$p(\Theta \mid X) = \frac{p(X \mid \Theta)p(\Theta)}{p(X)}$$
$$\propto p(X \mid \Theta)p(\Theta) \tag{3.7}$$

Since $p(X)$ is independent of Θ, it can be ignored. The MAP estimate Θ_{MAP} can be defined as,

$$\Theta_{MAP} = \arg\max_{\Theta} log \prod_t p(x_t \mid \Theta)p(\Theta) \tag{3.8}$$

The only difference in MLE (Equation 3.6) and MAP (Equation 3.8) is the inclusion of prior probability $p(\Theta)$ in MAP. In other words, the likelihood function is now weighted using some weight from the prior probability. Assuming that, the model is seeking its parameter values using MAP estimation with uniform prior probability (*i.e.*, equal prior probability), it assigns equal weight to each instance. This implies that the likelihood function is now weighted by some constant. Since any constant will not contribute in the maximization and can be dropped from MAP. Hence, they both are similar in this particular scenario. For a given feature set $X = \{x_t, t = 1, \ldots, T\}$ of T local descriptors, the soft assignment of descriptor x_t to the k-th cluster is defined as:

$$q_t(k) = \frac{w_k \mathcal{N}(x_t \mid \mu_k, \Sigma_k)}{\displaystyle\sum_{j=1}^{K} w_j \mathcal{N}(x_t \mid \mu_j, \Sigma_j)} \tag{3.9}$$

To build a codebook, the local motion descriptors are computed from the video sequences in training dataset and one million features are randomly selected from each local descriptor. It is assumed that each mixture component in a codebook represents a particular motion pattern shared by the local descriptors. Unlike the k-means clustering which performs a hard assignment of the feature descriptor to the component, GMM applies a soft assignment of the descriptor to the components. In this way, the local descriptors are assigned to various components in a weighted manner using the posterior component probability given by the descriptor. In the proposed technique, the model parameters are estimated using the Expectation Maximization (EM) algorithm [DLR77] which is an iterative technique to find the maximum likelihood or maximum a posterior estimates of the model parameters. It has two steps in each iteration: expectation and maximization. In the first step of expectation, the probability of each local descriptor belonging to the multiple components is computed using the current estimated mean (μ) and covariance ($\sum$), as depicted in Equation 3.9. The second step of maximization recalculate the weight (w), μ and $\sum$ based on the probabilities calculated in the expectation step. The algorithm iterates between these two steps until the parameters converge to some optimal values.

3.1.3   Feature Encoding

As described earlier, feature encoding is the transformation of local descriptors into a fixed length vector. Assuming that $X = \{x_t, t = 1, \ldots, T\} \in \mathbb{R}^{D \times T}$ is a set of D-dimensional local descriptors extracted from the video sequence and $C = \{c_k, k = 1, \ldots, K\} \in \mathbb{R}^{D \times K}$ is representing a codebook with K components, the aim of encoding is to compute the high-level representation of X using C. Generally, this process is accomplished by the vector quantization and building a histogram of visual words known as bag-of-visual-words [Pen+16]. However, inspired by the recent success of FV encoding in image classification and action recognition [Sán+13; Pen+14], the local descriptors in the proposed gait recognition algorithm are encoded using FV. This high level representation is based on the principle of Fisher kernel which combine the benefits of both generative and discriminative approaches. The key idea is to derive a kernel function from the generative probabilistic model (*i.e.*, GMM) and describe a natural comparison between the feature vectors induced by the GMM. In particular, Fisher kernel defines a Riemannian manifold with a local metric relation between the feature vectors to measure their similarities. In this way, the Euclidean distance between the feature vectors is obtained directly from the kernel function and can be used to describe the similarity between them [JH99].

The FV representation contains the deviation of local descriptors from the generative model by computing the gradient of the descriptor log-likelihood with respect to the model parameters. The gradient process describes the contribution of the individual parameters in the generation process. That is, it demonstrates that how the model-parameters can be altered to best fit the data. The gradient of the descriptor log-likelihood is also know as Fisher score and plays an important role in order to measure its similarity. Specifically, the Fisher kernel provides the mapping of the inner product between the feature vectors to the Riemannian manifold [JH99]. Since the inner product of the feature vectors implies a

Euclidean metric in the feature space by adopting the basic comparison between them, such a representation is also discriminative in nature. Moreover, such an explicit implementation states that Fisher vectors can alternatively be used with more sophisticated kernel-based classifier *e.g.* to determine the linear boundary in the feature space.

The encoding phase begins by learning the GMM and the local descriptors are transformed into a high-level representation using the probability density function $p(X|\Theta)$ (Equation 3.4). Specifically, for a given feature set $X = \{x_t, t = 1, \ldots, T\}$ from local descriptors, the FV representation F_X is constructed by computing the gradient vector of its log-likelihood function at current model parameter Θ. That is,

$$F_X = \frac{1}{T} \nabla_\Theta \log p(X|\Theta), \tag{3.10}$$

where ∇_Θ represents the gradient of the log-likelihood function which describes the contribution of parameters in the generation process. Assuming that x_t is a D-dimensional local descriptor, and the covariance matrices are diagonal and denoted by σ_k^2 the variance vector. The gradient vectors with respect to mean μ_k and standard deviation σ_k can be computed as [PSM10]:

$$u_k = \frac{1}{T \sqrt{w_k}} \sum_{t=1}^{T} q_t(k) \frac{x_t - \mu_k}{\sigma_k}, \tag{3.11}$$

$$v_k = \frac{1}{T \sqrt{2w_k}} \sum_{t=1}^{T} q_t(k) \left[\frac{(x_t - \mu_k)^2}{\sigma_k^2} - 1 \right], \tag{3.12}$$

where $q_t(k)$ is representing the soft assignment of the descriptor x_t to the k-th Gaussian component (Equation 3.9). Moreover, u_k and v_k are D-dimensional gradient vectors with respect to μ_k and σ_k, which are also known as respectively the first and second order differences of the local descriptor to the mixture components. The FV encoding of a local descriptor comprises the concatenation of u and v for all K components. Therefore, the size of FV representation would be $2KD$, where K is representing the total number of mixtures and D is the dimension of the descriptor. That is,

$$F = [u_1^\top, v_1^\top, u_2^\top, v_2^\top, u_3^\top, v_3^\top, \ldots, u_K^\top, v_K^\top]^\top \tag{3.13}$$

The local descriptors HOG, MBH_x and MBH_y are computed from the gait sequences in gallery and probe sets, and encoded using the above described formulation. Later, the proposed algorithm fused them using representation level fusion [Pen+16; Kha+17]. That is,

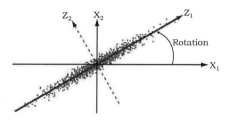

Figure 3.4: An illustration of PCA. The data points in original axes (*i.e.*, X_1 and X_2) are assumed to be strongly correlated. Applying PCA projects them in new principal axes (*i.e.*, Z_1 and Z_2). The first principal component Z_1 contains the highest variance of the data.

each local descriptor is encoded into FV representation, separately and their concatenation yields a final gait representation.

3.1.4 Dimensionality Reduction

The process of dimensionality reduction consists of mapping the original high-dimensional data onto a compact low-dimensional space. Principal Component Analysis (PCA) has been used in several statistical and machine learning based applications to get the reduced but compact representation of the original data. It transforms the possible correlated variables into a small number of uncorrelated variables. In particular, PCA aims to construct a matrix of possibly correlated n instances with d dimension of each, and summarize it by uncorrelated dimensions known as principal components. Usually, few number of principal components are employed to represent the data which is much less than the actual number of variables in the original data, thus it results in dimension reduction. Graphically, this process can be achieved by rotating the original d dimensional axes to the new principal axes, so that the first principal axis comprises the highest variance of the data, the second axis contains the second highest and so forth. In general the first few principal components comprise the most of the information of data, therefore the rest of the components can be dropped to reduce the dimension. Figure 3.4 depicts the process of dimensionality reduction on 2D data, where the data is projected using new principal axes Z_1 and Z_2. It can be seen that principal axis Z_1 comprises the highest variability in the data, whereas Z_2 comprises very low variability of the data, and therefore may dropped. The several usages of PCA include data compression and visualization, noise reduction, efficient classification, *etc.* The other advantages also include efficient storage and less computation power to process the reduced dimensional data.

The proposed algorithm employs PCA at computed gait descriptors to evaluate their impact in the recognition accuracy and the detailed analysis is presented in Section 3.2.2.

3.1.5 Classification

Recall that the similarity between two samples X and Y can be measured using the Fisher kernel (FK) which is defined as the dot-product between the feature vectors of X and Y. That is,

$$FK(X,Y) = F'_X \cdot F_Y, \tag{3.14}$$

where F_X and F_Y are representing the FV for samples X and Y, respectively. In other words, any non-linear kernel machine using FK as kernel would be the same as a linear kernel machine using F_X as feature vector. Therefore, based on such an explicit formulation any simple linear classifier can be learned very efficiently.

The proposed gait recognition algorithm employs a simple linear Support Vector Machine (SVM) to classify the spatiotemporal gait descriptors. Specifically, it exploits the implementation of LIBLINEAR SVM library[1]. SVM has been used as a powerful classification tool in many computer vision-based applications. It has been proven an efficient solution for the classification of large sparse dataset with an enormous number of examples and features [Fan+08a]. SVM first maps the training instances into high dimensional space, and then extracts a decision boundary (*e.g.* hyperplane) between the instances of different classes based on the principle of maximizing the margin (*i.e.*, the distance between the hyperplane and the nearest data point in each class is maximized). For example, consider a case of a two-class classification problem where a given set of labeled training instances $(x_i, y_i), x_i \in \mathbb{R}$ and $y_i = \{-1, +1\}$ is provided. That is, the positive instances are associated with label $y_i = +1$, the negative instances have labels $y_i = -1$. The training process aims to find such a hyperplane which should be in the middle of positive and negative instances, and the distance of hyperplane with the nearest positive and negative instances should be maximized. Mathematically, to determine this hyperplane between a set of objects having different classes, the following optimization problem is solved,

$$\min_{w} \quad \frac{1}{2}\|w\|^2 + C\sum_{i=1}^{N} \xi_i \tag{3.15}$$
$$s.t. \quad y_i(w^T x_i + b) \geq 1 - \xi_i, \qquad \xi_i \geq 0, \qquad \forall i$$

---

[1]https://www.csie.ntu.edu.tw/~cjlin/liblinear/

where $\xi_i = max(0, 1 - y_i w^T x_i)^2$ is known as L_2 loss function. Moreover, w is representing the weight vector and $C > 0$ is a penalty parameter for the classification error. It is to be noted that the objective is to maximize the margin, *i.e.*, minimizing the regularization term $\|w\|^2$ augmented with a term $C \sum_{i=1}^{N} \xi_i$ to penalize the classification and margin errors. The soft margin parameter C plays a vital role in maximizing the margin and minimizing the loss function. To validate the model with the selection of C, the proposed technique performed 10-fold cross validation prior to training the actual model on the full training database. To solve the multi-class problem, it employs the one-vs-rest strategy.

3.1.6 Experiments and Results

In order to assess the performance of the proposed gait recognition algorithm, an extensive experimental evaluation is carried out on five large benchmark gait databases: CMU MoBo [GS01], CASIA-A [Wan+03b], CASIA-B [Yu+06], CASIA-C [Tan+06], and TUM GAID [HBR12]. Each database comprises the gait sequences with several variations in walking styles, speed, clothing, *etc.* For example, TUM GIAD gait database consists of three variations in walking styles, namely: normal walk, walk with backpack, and walk with coating shoes. Moreover, the recording was held in two different seasons, therefore the significant variations in clothing and environment can be observed. Table 3.1 presents the summary of gait databases, used in experimental evaluation. In each database, the codebook is computed separately using the local motion descriptors of training dataset. Specifically, one million local descriptors are randomly selected to build a codebook with GMM, which is later used to encode the FV. The mixture components K in GMM are empirically computed and set to 2^8 in all experiments. To compare the recognition accuracies with existing methods, the same distribution of gallery and probe sets is used.

Performance evaluation on CASIA-A gait database

The CASIA-A gait database contains the gait sequences of 20 subjects. There are four walk sequences for each subject, recorded under three different viewing angles: 0° (*i.e.*, lateral view), 45° (*i.e.*, oblique view) and 90° (*i.e.*, frontal view). Each subject walks twice, from left-to-right and from right-to-left. The evaluation of the proposed technique is carried out on the sequences recorded in lateral view. Two sample images from the database in lateral view are presented in Figure 3.5. In experimental setting, the first three sequences of each subject are used to form a gallery set and the remaining one is used in the probe set. The recognition result and its comparison with existing methods are reported in Table 3.2. The proposed method obtained the highest recognition rate of 100% on CASIA-A gait database.

Table 3.1: Summary of gait databases used in performance evaluation. Size represents the number of gait video sequences in the database used in experimental evaluation.

Database	Size	Walk Scenarios
CASIA-A	80	Left-to-right walk, right-to-left walk
CMU MoBo	300	Slow walk, fast walk, slow walk with ball in hands, slow walk at certain slope
CASIA-B	1,240	Normal walk, walk with bag, walk with coat
CASIA-C	1,530	Normal walk, slow walk, fast walk, walk with back-pack
TUM GAID	3,370	Left-to-right and right-to-left walk with three variations: normal walk, walk with backpack, walk with coating shoes

(a)   (b)

Figure 3.5: Example images from CASIA-A gait database. (a) Left to right walk and (b) right to left walk in a lateral view.

Table 3.2: Comparison of recognition accuracy (%) on CASIA-A gait database. The best result is marked in bold.

Method	Accuracy
Wavelet descriptors+ICA [LZJ06]	82.5
Partial silhouette [SSC14]	85.0
PSC [Kus+11a]	97.5
NN [LHK08]	87.5
2D polar-plane [CG07]	92.5
Method [Wu+07]	90.0
Method [Gen+07]	90.0
PSA [Wan+03a]	88.8
Curves+NN [SH06]	89.3
STC+PCA [Wan+03b]	82.5
GEI [Niz+08]	95.0
Proposed	**100.0**

Performance evaluation on CASIA-B gait database

The CASIA-B is one of the large database contain the walk sequences of 124 subjects, recorded from 11 different viewing angles. Each subject has three different variations in walking style, namely: normal walk (*nm*), walk with bag (*bg*) and walk with coat (*cl*). There are ten walking sequences for each subject: six sequences of normal walk and two sequences for each of the rest. The evaluation of the proposed algorithm is carried out on the sequences recorded in lateral view. Few sample images from the database illustrating the three variations of walk in lateral view are presented in Figure 3.6. The proposed algorithm is evaluated on this database to demonstrate its robustness and effectiveness against the variations in clothing

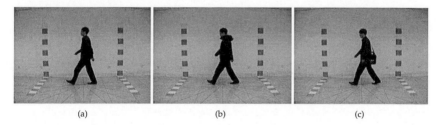

(a)   (b)   (c)

Figure 3.6: Sample images from CASIA-B database. (a) Normal walk, (b) walk with coat and (c) walk with bag in a lateral view.

Table 3.3: Comparison of recognition accuracies (%) on CASIA-B gait database. Each column of *nm*, *bg* and *cl* corresponds to a different experiment. 'Avg' represents the average performance of each method in all three experiments. The best results are marked in bold.

Experiment	*nm*	*bg*	*cl*	Avg
TM [BXG08]	97.6	52.0	32.7	60.8
GEI [Wan+12]	91.6	31.7	24.0	49.1
CGI [Wan+12]	88.0	43.7	43.0	58.2
iHMM [Hu+13a]	94.0	45.2	42.9	60.7
AEI+2DLPP [ZZX10]	98.4	91.9	72.2	87.5
Baseline method [Yu+06]	97.6	52.0	32.2	60.8
GEnI [BXG09]	98.3	80.1	33.5	70.7
RF+FSS+CDA [DSV13]	100.0	50.0	33.1	61.0
HSD [Kus14]	94.5	62.9	58.1	71.8
M_j+ACDA [BXG08]	100.0	91.0	80.0	90.3
DCS+H2M [CMJG16]	100.0	99.2	72.6	90.6
SDL [ZWY14]	98.4	93.5	**90.3**	94.1
Proposed	**100.0**	**100.0**	89.9	**96.6**

and carrying a bag during the walk. In experimental setting, the first four sequences of normal walk from all 124 subjects are used to form a gallery set. The remaining two sequences of normal walk, walk with bag and walk with wearing a coat are placed in a probe set separately to conduct three different experiments, namely: *nm*, *bg* and *cl*. Table 3.3 presents the recognition accuracies achieved by the proposed algorithm and their comparisons with other well-known gait recognition techniques. The results show that the proposed algorithm outperforms others in *nm* and *bg*, while SDL [ZWY14] performs slightly better in *cl* than the proposed algorithm. Overall, it achieved the highest average recognition rate of 96.6%.

Performance evaluation on CASIA-C database

The CASIA-C database comprises the gait sequences of 153 subjects with four variations in walk, namely: normal walk (*fn*), slow walk (*fs*), fast walk (*fq*), and walk with backpack (*fb*). Each subject in the database has four sequences of *fn* and two sequences of each *fs*, *fq* and *fb*. The database is recorded at night using a low resolution thermal camera. Figure 3.7 presents few sample images from the database to illustrate the variations in walking style and illumination condition. The aim of evaluating the performance of gait recognition algorithms on this database is to verify their robustness under variations in the walking speed, carrying condition and illumination changes. In experimental setting, three

| (a) | (b) | (c) | (d) |

Figure 3.7: Sample images from CASIA-C database. (a) Normal walk, (b) slow walk, (c) fast walk and (d) walk with backpack.

sequences of fn from all 153 subjects are used to form a gallery set. In the first experiment, the remaining fourth sequence of fn is placed in a probe set. Moreover, in the next three experiments, the sequences of fs, fq and fb are placed in a probe set separately, while the gallery set remains the same. Table 3.4 presents the recognition accuracies achieved by the proposed algorithm and their comparison with the state-of-the-art techniques. The results show that the proposed algorithm outperforms the existing methods in fn, fb and fs experiments and achieves the highest average recognition rate of 99.8%.

Table 3.4: Comparison of recognition accuracies (%) on CASIA-C gait database. fn, fs, fq and fb correspond to the different experiments. 'Avg' represents the average performance of each method. The best results are marked in bold.

Experiment	fn	fs	fq	fb	Avg
AEI+2DLPP [ZZX10]	88.9	89.2	90.2	79.7	87.0
WBP [Kus+09a]	99.0	86.4	89.6	80.7	88.9
NDDP [Tan+07d]	97.0	83.0	83.0	17.0	70.0
OP [Tan+07a]	98.0	80.0	80.0	16.0	68.5
HSD [Kus14]	97.0	86.0	89.0	65.0	84.2
Wavelet packet [DASZ09]	93.0	83.0	85.0	21.0	70.5
Pseudo shape [Tan+07b]	98.4	91.3	93.7	24.7	77.03
Gait curves [DR10]	91.0	65.4	69.9	25.5	62.9
HTI [Tan+06]	94.0	85.0	88.0	51.0	79.5
Uniprojective [Tan+07c]	97.0	84.0	88.0	37.0	76.5
RSM [GL13]	100.0	**99.7**	99.6	96.2	98.9
SDL [ZWY14]	95.4	91.2	92.5	81.7	90.2
PFM [Cas+17]	100.0	98.7	100.0	99.3	99.5
Proposed	**100.0**	99.4	**100.0**	**100.0**	**99.8**

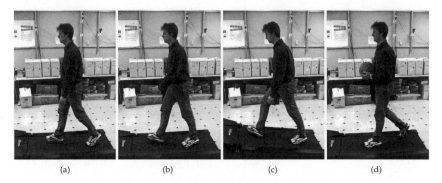

Figure 3.8: Sample images from CMU MoBo database. (a) Slow walk, (b) fast walk, (c) walk at certain slope (*i.e.*, incline) and (d) slow walk with ball.

Performance evaluation on CMU MoBo database

The CMU MoBo database contains the gait sequences of 25 subjects walking on a treadmill. Each subject has four different variations of walk, namely: slow walk (*S*), fast walk (*F*), slow walk with ball in hands (*B*) and slow walk at certain slope (*I*) *i.e.*, incline. The video sequences are recorded using 6 cameras distributed evenly around the treadmill to capture the walk with different viewing angles. However, the proposed algorithm is evaluated on the sequences recorded in lateral view to asses its performance in dealing with the variations in walking speed, walking surface (*i.e.*, incline), and carrying objects during the walk. Few sample images from the database representing the variations in walking styles in lateral view are presented in Figure 3.8. Similar to [ZWY14], the video sequences are divided into three equal parts to increase the number of instances in gallery and probe sets. Two different types of experiments are conducted, (1) same scenario, where the similar walking scenarios are used in gallery and probe sets, and (2) across the scenario, where diverse walking scenarios are used in gallery and probe sets.

Table 3.5 describes the summary of sixteen experiments on this database. Table 3.6 presents the recognition accuracies achieved by the proposed algorithm and their comparison with existing state-of-the-art techniques. The results show that the proposed algorithm outperforms all existing methods in all experiments except experiment *G* where PFM [Cas+17] performs better than the proposed method. Overall, the proposed method achieves the highest average recognition rate of 98.5%.

Table 3.5: Summary of sixteen experiments on CMU MoBo gait database. The column 'Exp.'
is representing the experiment number.

Same scenario			Across scenario		
Exp.	Gallery set	Probe set	Exp.	Gallery set	Probe set
A	Slow walk	Slow walk	E	Slow walk	Fast walk
B	Fast walk	Fast walk	F	Slow walk	Walk at an incline
C	Walk with ball	Walk with ball	G	Slow walk	Walk with ball
D	Walk at an incline	Walk at an incline	H	Fast walk	Slow walk
			I	Fast walk	Walk at an incline
			J	Fast walk	Walk with ball
			K	Walk with ball	Slow walk
			L	Walk with ball	Fast walk
			M	Walk with ball	Walk at an incline
			N	Walk at an incline	Slow walk
			O	Walk at an incline	Slow walk
			P	Walk at an incline	Walk with ball

Performance evaluation on TUM GAID database

TUM GAID is another large gait database which contains the 3,370 gait sequences of 305
subjects, recorded in an outdoor environment of Technical University of Munich, Germany.
The database was recorded in two different seasons, using a Microsoft Kinect camera. The
first recording was held in January 2012, and the gait sequences of 176 subjects were captured.
Since it was winter at that time with an average temperature around -5°C, the subjects were
wearing heavy jackets and winter boots. The second part of the database was recorded
in April 2012, and the gait sequences of 161 subjects were captured. During the second
recording, the average temperature was around +15°C in the region and the subjects were
wearing significantly different clothes. There is subset of 32 subjects who took part in
both recordings and thus, in total the database contains the walk sequences of 305 subjects.
Consequently, a significant variation in the clothing and appearance of the participants
can be observed (Figure 3.9). The database comprises the ten sequences of walk for each
subject with three variations, namely normal walk (N), walk with backpack (B) and walk
with coating shoes (S). Each subject has six sequences of N and two sequences for each of
the rest. The subset of 32 subjects (who participated in both recordings) has ten additional
walk sequences (*i.e.*, in total 20 sequences) namely: normal walk after time (TN), walk
with backpack after time (TB) and walk with coating shoes after time (TS). The significant

Table 3.6: Comparison of recognition accuracies (%) on CMU MoBo gait database. Each column corresponds to a different experiment and 'Avg' represents the average performances of the methods which are reported in all experiments. The best results are marked in bold. Note that hyphen (-) means that either the results are not available or the respective approach cannot be evaluated under those experiments.

Methods	A	B	C	D	E	F	G	H	I	J	K	L	M	N	O	P	Avg
SC [VRCC05]	100.0	100.0	92.0	92.0	80.0	48.0	48.0	84.0	28.0	48.0	68.0	48.0	28.0	32.0	44.0	20.0	60.0
Partial silhouette [SSC14]	88.0	88.0	-	-	32.0	-	-	28.0	-	-	-	-	-	-	-	-	59.0
ICA [Lia+06]	100.0	100.0	100.0	100.0	-	-	79.2	64.0	-	-	-	-	-	-	-	-	90.5
SSP [BCD04]	100.0	100.0	-	-	54.0	-	-	32.0	-	-	-	-	-	-	-	-	71.5
Eigen features [Kal+03]	95.8	95.8	95.4	-	-	-	-	75.0	-	-	-	-	-	-	-	-	90.5
HMM [Kal+04]	72.0	68.0	91.0	-	56.0	-	-	59.0	-	-	-	-	-	-	-	-	69.2
Shape kinematics [VCC04]	100.0	100.0	92.0	92.0	80.0	48.0	48.0	84.0	28.0	48.0	68.0	48.0	12.0	32.0	44.0	20.0	59.0
PFM [Cas+17]	-	-	-	-	92.0	100.0	100.0	92.0	96.0	83.3	48.0	48.0	44.0	100.0	96.0	87.5	82.2
GEI [Siv+11b]	100.0	100.0	100.0	-	95.0	-	80.0	-	-	-	-	70.0	-	-	-	-	90.8
STM-SPP [CT12]	100.0	100.0	100.0	-	94.0	-	93.0	91.0	-	84.0	82.0	82.0	-	-	-	-	91.8
3D ellipsoid [Siv+11a]	100.0	100.0	100.0	-	78.6	-	70.5	-	-	-	-	61.0	-	-	-	-	85.1
WBP [Kus+09a]	100.0	100.0	100.0	98.67	92.0	-	72.67	92.0	-	60.67	74.67	63.33	-	-	-	-	85.4
Uniprojective [Tan+07c]	100.0	100.0	96.0	-	72.0	-	-	60.0	-	-	-	-	-	-	-	-	85.6
NDDP [Tan+07d]	100.0	100.0	96.0	-	88.0	-	-	80.0	-	-	-	-	-	-	-	-	92.8
HSD [Kus14]	100.0	100.0	100.0	-	92.0	-	-	-	-	-	88.0	84.0	-	-	-	-	94.0
SDL [ZWY14]	100.0	100.0	98.7	-	96.0	-	86.7	92.0	-	88.0	86.7	88.0	-	-	-	-	92.9
Proposed	**100.0**	**100.0**	**100.0**	**100.0**	**100.0**	**100.0**	**96.0**	**100.0**	**100.0**	**96.0**	**96.0**	**96.0**	**96.0**	**100.0**	**100.0**	**96.0**	**98.5**

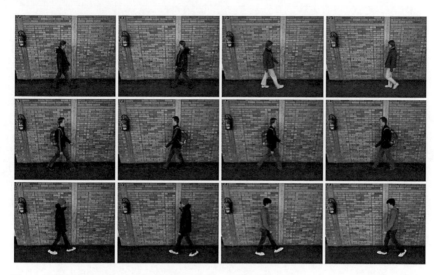

Figure 3.9: Sample images from TUM GAID gait database. Top row: normal walk, middle row: walk with backpack, and bottom row: walk with coating shoes. The first two images of each row represent the walk sequences (from left-to-right and right-to-left), captured in the first recording and the remaining two images are captured in the second recoding for the same subject.

differences in clothing, lighting and other captured properties due to time variation make this database challenging in the field of gait recognition.

The proposed algorithm employs the similar distribution of database, as defined in [HBR12]. The database is distributed into two parts: (1) the development set which contains the walk sequences of 150 subjects; (2) test set which comprises the walk successions of 155 subjects. The development set is used to compute a codebook and the test set is employed to construct the gallery and probe sets to assess the performance of the proposed algorithm. Similar to [HBR12], the first four sequences of N from each subject (i.e., $N_1 - N_4$) are used to form a gallery set. In the first set of three experiments, namely N, B and S, the rest of $N_5 - N_6, B_1 - B_2$, and $S_1 - S_2$ are used in probe sets, separately. Furthermore, in the next three experiments namely TN, TB and TS, the rest of $N_7 - N_8, B_3 - B_4$ and $S_3 - S_4$ are used in probe sets separately, while the gallery set is the same as in the previous experiments. It is worth mentioning that the TUM GAID database also provides the cropped RGB and depth frames along with the human detection; however, the proposed algorithm employed full

Table 3.7: Comparison of recognition accuracies (%) on TUM GAID database. Each column N, B, S, TN, TB and TS corresponds to a different experiment. The column 'Avg' represents the average performance of the method. Best results are marked in bold.

Method	N	B	S	TN	TB	TS	Avg
GEI [HBR12]	99.4	27.1	56.2	44.0	6.0	9.0	56.0
GEV [HBR12]	94.2	13.9	87.7	41.0	0.0	31.0	61.4
SEIM [WBR14]	99.0	18.4	96.1	15.6	3.1	28.1	66.0
GVI [WBR14]	99.0	47.7	94.5	62.5	15.6	62.5	77.3
SVIM [WBR14]	98.4	64.2	91.6	65.6	31.3	50.0	81.4
DGHEI [HBR12]	99.0	40.3	96.1	50.0	0.0	44.0	87.3
CNN-SVM [Cas+16]	99.7	97.1	97.1	59.4	50.0	**62.5**	94.2
CNN-NN128 [Cas+16]	99.7	98.1	95.8	62.5	56.3	59.4	94.2
H2M [CMJG16]	99.4	100.0	98.1	71.9	63.4	43.8	95.5
PFM [Cas+17]	99.7	99.0	99.0	**78.1**	62.0	54.9	96.0
Proposed	**99.7**	**100.0**	**99.7**	68.8	**71.9**	53.1	**96.5**

frame video sequences in all experiments. The recognition results achieved by the proposed algorithm and their comparison with state-of-the-art techniques are presented in Table 3.7. It can be shown that the proposed algorithm outperforms all competing methods in the first set of experiments N, B and S with a recognition accuracy of 99.7%, 100% and 99.7%, respectively. Moreover, in the next set of three experiments the proposed algorithm performs best in TB experiment achieving 71.9% recognition accuracy, whereas, PFM [Cas+17] and CNN-SVM [Cas+16] perform better than the proposed method in TN and TS experiments, respectively. Overall, the proposed algorithm achieved the best average recognition accuracy of 96.5%.

It is worth to mention that most of the existing gait recognition algorithms usually evaluate their methods either at one or two databases containing some specific walk scenarios. However, a rigorous evaluation of the proposed algorithm is carried using five large benchmark gait databases with several variations in the walking styles. The recognition accuracies reported in Table 3.2 – 3.7 demonstrate that the proposed gait recognition algorithm performs consistently better than many existing state-of-the-art techniques on these five gait databases. The proposed gait representation is proven to be robust against the variations in walk due to clothing, shoes, backpacks, bags, walking surface, speed, illumination and *etc*. The reason for the higher recognition rate of the proposed gait representation is that it is not dependent either on the localization or the segmentation of human body region from the images. Moreover, it neither requires the prior information of human body shape nor the gait cycle estimation. One can observe that an inaccurate localization/segmentation of the human body region in existing techniques may disrupt the process of gait construction and ultimately degrade the performance of the respective technique. However, the proposed gait representation is free from such a limitations and can be computed directly from the video sequences. It achieved the highest average recognition accuracies in each of the afore-mentioned benchmark database using only a simple linear SVM, which also demonstrate the discriminative strength of the proposed gait representation.

3.2 Adaptation of Generic Codebook for Gait Recognition Algorithms

A codebook is an effective mean to describe the contents, structures, and layouts of a dataset. Numerous recognition based approaches have been proposed that exploit the codebooks to encode the image/video sequences. Such approaches use a subset of the dataset to construct a codebook which is then used to encode the rest of the sequences in the dataset, *i.e.*, the codebooks are dataset specific. This section explores the idea of using a generic codebook for gait recognition. The concept can be extended in the encoding of any local descriptors which are based on codebook approach.

In general, the codebooks are application specific and built using a subset of the target dataset, known as training set. The concept of building a *generic codebook* aims at constructing a single codebook using one dataset and adopt it to encode the image/video sequences of other datasets. Since a codebook is directly involved in the encoding of sequences, the selection of dataset to build a generic codebook is important in the efficient encoding and recognition accuracy of the algorithm. For gait recognition, a database with diverse walking styles is required to encode the gait sequences efficiently. The encoding of gait descriptor using a codebook computed from the limited walking styles may ignore some important cues, resulting in poor performance [KFG18b].

To this end, an investigation of the existing git datasets is carried out and a subset of CMU Motion Capture (mocap) database [Cmu] is selected to generate a generic codebook. It contains a total of 80 synthetic video sequences of walk which cover a large variety of walking styles including normal walk, variations in speed, exaggerated stride, brisk walk, wander, *etc.* Few sample images of normal walk from the selected dataset are shown in Figure 3.10.

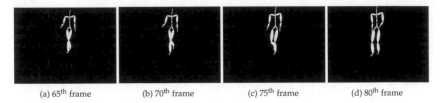

(a) 65th frame   (b) 70th frame   (c) 75th frame   (d) 80th frame

Figure 3.10: Sample images from a synthetic gait sequence of normal walk in mocap dataset.

3.2.1 Experiments and Results

To build a generic codebook, the local motion descriptors are computed from the selected synthetic gait sequences of mocap, as described in Section 3.1.1. Then, one million local descriptors are randomly selected from each descriptor and used to build a generic codebook, as illustrated in Section 3.1.2. It is worth mentioning that the proposed generic codebook only employs the motion descriptors from synthetic gait sequences of mocap, and it does not use any real gait sequences of gallery or probe set from any other database. The experimental evaluation is carried out on the same five gait databases, which were evaluated by the gait recognition algorithm defined in Section 3.1. The local descriptors of all five gait databases are encoded using the generic codebook, and classified using linear SVM. The recognition accuracies in comparison with a database-specific codebook is illustrated in Figure 3.11.

The results show that the proposed gait recognition algorithm with generic codebook performs quite well and the idea of generic codebook is effective. In comparison with database-specific codebooks, the average difference of recognition rate is dropped around 1%. Despite of this small loss in recognition accuracy, the generic codebook possesses numerous advantages, *e.g.* since it is computed only once to be used for all databases rather than to compute for each database, it is computationally efficient and requires less storage. Moreover, the generic codebook is computed using the diversity of walking styles, it can be adopted as a universal codebook. That is, any kind of individual's walk can be encoded efficiently using it. However, this would not be the case with database-specific codebook approach. Since one database consists of few particular walk scenarios, any probable changes in the dataset (*e.g.* new walking styles) would require the re-computation of codebook.

3.2.2 Discussion

The impact of dimensionality reduction is quantitatively assessed in the recognition accuracy, computational complexity and the space requirement of the proposed spatiotemporal gait descriptors. Since the higher dimensional features require higher computational com-

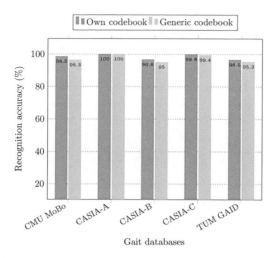

Figure 3.11: Performance comparison of the recognition accuracies on all five gait databases with database-specific codebook and the generic codebook.

plexity and more storage requirement, PCA is employed to transform the higher dimensional gait descriptors into the compact and low dimensional space by preserving the maximum possible variance of the data. Assuming that d is the dimension of the proposed gait descriptor which is $2KD$; where K is the mixture components and D is the dimension of local descriptors (having values 256 and 96, respectively). Since d is quite large, the size of the proposed descriptor is empirically computed and set to 2,000. This process prompts a simple model learning and delivers more discriminative features for gait recognition. The comparison of recognition results achieved by the proposed gait recognition algorithm on full-length gait descriptors and PCA reduced-length descriptors is presented in Figure 3.12. The recognition results reveal that the reduced-length gait descriptors perform significantly better (up to 27% higher) than the full-length descriptors. The analysis of dimensionality reduction is also carried out on the computation time and the memory requirement of the proposed gait descriptors. The execution time for the classification (in seconds) and the memory utilization (in Megabytes) of the gait descriptors before and after applying PCA are computed. Table 3.8 presents the percentage of memory saving and the speedup gain due to PCA. It can be concluded from the results that applying PCA with the proposed gait descriptors not only improves their discriminative power, but also significantly reduces the classification time and memory requirement.

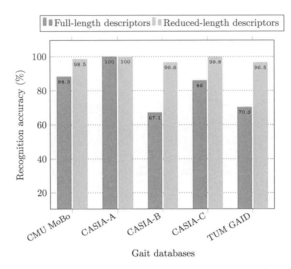

Figure 3.12: Performance comparison of the recognition results on all five gait databases using full-length and reduced-length gait descriptors.

Table 3.8: Analysis of classification time and space requirement of the proposed algorithm on full-length and reduced-length gait descriptors. *MB* is representing the Megabytes and *Sec* is seconds.

Database	Size (MB)			Time (Sec)		
	Full	Reduced	% Saving	Full	Reduced	% Speedup
CMU MoBo	164.70	3.4	97.94	12.65	0.14	98.89
CASIA-A	71.90	1.80	97.50	7.20	0.51	92.91
CASIA-B	917.70	20.10	97.81	1330.30	13.67	98.97
CASIA-C	2252.80	29.00	98.71	2666.98	35.56	98.67
TUM GAID	1638.40	30.5	98.14	2068.16	27.71	98.66
Average	-	-	98.02	-	-	97.62

3.3 Summary

This chapter introduced a spatiotemporal gait representation which employed the motion characteristics of an individual's walk. Two techniques are proposed to construct the gait descriptors with the aim that they neither require the segmentation of human body region nor gait cycle estimation. In Section 3.1, a gait recognition framework is presented which compute the local motion descriptors directly from the video sequences. The local descriptors are encoded using a codebook based on GMM and FV encoding. The classification is carried out using simple linear SVM. Subsequently, Section 3.2 presents an idea of generic codebook, which is computed once and can be used to encode the gait sequences of any database. The experimental evaluations of both techniques are carried out on five large bench mark gait databases and their recognition results are discussed. Finally, the impact of generic codebook and dimensionality reduction is also analyzed in the recognition accuracy of the proposed gait recognition algorithm.

Chapter 4

Cross-view Gait Recognition

Gait recognition is affected by many covariate factors, such as clothing, walking surface, walking speed, carrying objects during the walk, illumination and viewing angle. Among these, the change in viewpoint is the most challenging and unavoidable factor in real-world surveillance systems because the appearance of an individual's walk changes significantly due to the change in the viewing angle. It introduces intra-personal variations which are always larger than inter-personal variations caused by others covariate factors [Wu+17]. Studies have shown that the single-view based recognition methods ignoring the variations of viewing angles may fail when the viewpoint changes. For example, the authors in [WRB06] have reported a recognition rate of 80% on INRIA Xmas Motion Acquisition Sequences dataset. However, the recognition rate dropped to 20% when evaluated in [FT08] under different viewpoints. A similar negative impact in the recognition rate of many gait recognition algorithms has been observed, as reported in [YTT06] where a classical GEI approach is evaluated under different viewpoints. Thus, gait recognition under varying viewing angle is a challenging problem compared to the single-view based gait recognition. This problem is generally handled by normalizing the gait descriptors computed from the walk sequences of different viewpoints prior to measuring their similarity.

The concept of view transformation has proven to be effective to deal with the cross-view variations as compared to other approaches [Kus+12a]. Such approaches do not require temporally synchronized gait images from the multiple calibrated cameras therefore they are suitable for real-world applications. VTM based approaches learn a mapping between the gait descriptors obtained from different viewpoints. The learned relationship is then used to construct the cross-view representation of test gait descriptors before measuring their similarity. Typically, the learning process of the VTM based approaches is carried out using the training data which consists of view-pairs appearing in gallery and probe sets. Later, the test gait descriptors from these two viewpoints are projected onto a common subspace using

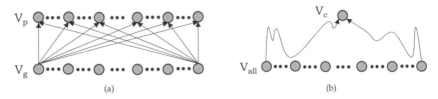

Figure 4.1: Example images illustrating the mapping between different viewpoints. (a) A linear view-pairs mapping of gallery and probe sets, (b) non-linear mapping between all the source viewpoints to the single canonical view. V_g, V_p, V_{all} and V_c are representing the sequences of gallery view, probe view, all viewing angles, and canonical view respectively.

the learned model, and their similarities are measured. However, such approaches [BXG10a; Kus+14; Mak+06; Kus+09b] construct multiple VTMs to learn a mapping between the different view-pairs of gallery and probe sets, as depicted in the Figure 4.1a. Moreover, most of VTM based approaches [Wu+17; YZC15] require segmented silhouette based gait representation (*e.g.* GEI) to learn the mapping of gait sequences from one view to another view creating a dependence on the segmentation accuracy. Although several efforts *e.g.* [Mak+15] have been made to refine the segmented silhouette shape for gait recognition; however, it is still a challenging problem in the literature.

To cope with the aforementioned limitations, a cross-view gait recognition technique is proposed in this chapter. The proposed technique extends the spatiotemporal gait representation (**Chapter 3**) for cross-view gait recognition. Instead of constructing a large number of VTMs for each view-pairs, the proposed technique learns a single model to map the gait sequences from multiple viewpoints to a single canonical view (Figure 4.1b). In particular, a deep neural network is constructed which learns a single model using all the gait descriptors obtained from different viewpoints and find a common high-level virtual path to project them on a single canonical view. The learning process does not require any viewpoint information of the descriptors. The proposed technique operate in three steps. In the first step, the spatiotemporal gait descriptors are directly computed from the video sequences. In the second step, a deep neural network is trained to map the gait descriptors obtained from all different possible viewpoints to a single canonical view. It is worth mentioning here that the training process of the proposed network is carried out only once for all the viewpoints, and it is based on the perception that the gait characteristics of an individual from different viewpoints have a common structure which makes it different from others. Therefore, the gait related features should be separated from the view related features which is not linearly possible [Kha+18b]. In the last step, the gait descriptors of gallery and probe sets

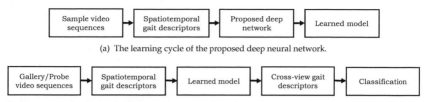

(a) The learning cycle of the proposed deep neural network.

(b) Cross-view gait recognition. The learning process of a single model to map the gait sequences from multiple viewpoints to a single canonical view is shown in (a).

Figure 4.2: Schematic diagram of the proposed cross-view gait recognition algorithm.

are propagated through the trained network and their cross-view representation is obtained which can be used for cross-view gait recognition. The gallery sequences (*i.e.*, cross-view gait descriptors) with their respective labels are used to train a classifier and the probe sequences are fed to the trained classifier for individual recognition. The proposed technique employs simple linear SVM [Fan+08a] as classifier to demonstrate the strength of cross-view gait descriptors. A block diagram representing the entire process of the proposed method is shown in Figure 4.2. The detail of each step of the proposed technique is presented in the following sections.

4.1 Gait Representation

In Chapter 3, a spatiotemporal based gait representation is presented which does not require any human body segmentation from the images/video. Since it is already shown in Section 3.1.6 that the spatiotemporal based gait representation has achieved excellent recognition accuracies in single-view gait recognition on various gait databases therefore, the proposed technique employed the same gait representation for cross-view gait recognition. That is, the local motion descriptors are computed from the video sequences using dense trajectories (Section 3.1.1) and their high-level representation is obtained using a codebook based on Gaussian mixture model and Fisher vector encoding, as described in Section 3.1.2–3.1.3.

4.2 View Transfer Model

A Non-linear Deep Neural Network (NDNN) is constructed in the proposed cross-view gait recognition algorithm to transfer the knowledge of gait descriptors obtained from different viewpoints to a single canonical view. The strength of the proposed NDNN is that it learns a single model for all the viewpoints by transforming the gait descriptors from any source viewpoint to the same canonical view, regardless of its input view. In particular, the input to the proposed NDNN is the spatiotemporal gait descriptors from all possible different source viewpoints. These gait descriptors are directly computed from the video sequences using dense trajectories, as described in Section 3.1.1– 3.1.3. Similarly, during the training the output to the proposed NDNN is the spatiotemporal gait descriptors from the canonical viewpoint. Thus, the proposed network tries to learn a set of transformations to map the gait descriptors of an individual from different source viewpoints to the same canonical view. Although any arbitrary viewpoint can be used as canonical view; however, the proposed algorithm exploits the side-view (*i.e.*, lateral-view) walking sequences as a canonical view. Later, the learned model is exploited to obtain a corresponding canonical view representation of any gait descriptor (*i.e.*, cross-view gait representation). Figure 4.3a illustrate the process of transforming the knowledge of gait descriptors from different source viewpoints to the same canonical view.

To map the gait descriptors from source to target viewpoint, the majority of existing cross-view gait recognition techniques *e.g.* [Mak+06; Kus+09b; Hu13; Kus+14; ZT05; Hu+13b] employed a set of linear transformations as depicted in Figure 4.1a. Thus, they cannot capture the non-linear manifolds where the realistic gait scenario may lie [Wu+17], for example when the gait sequence is obtained from different viewpoint. To conquer this issue, a multi-step virtual path is learned in the proposed NDNN using a set of non-linear transformations of gait descriptors to map the different source viewpoints to the same canonical view. Following this way, the source viewpoints are mapped to intermediate virtual views along the non-linear path prior to construct the final canonical view [Kha+18b; RMS17]. In particular, the virtual views can be obtained using the transformations of gait descriptor. The learning of the proposed NDNN is based on two perceptions: First, the gait sequences of an individual obtained from different viewpoints incorporate the same high-level characteristics which make them distinct from the rest. Second, for m different source viewpoints there would be m different virtual paths connecting them to the canonical view, where each virtual path is a set of non-linear transformations of gait descriptors [Kha+18b]. With these perceptions, the aim of the proposed network is to learn a single non-linear virtual path which encodes the common high-level characteristics of gait descriptors in the path by connecting the source viewpoint to the canonical view. That is, the learning process forces the m different virtual paths to concede on a single virtual path as presented in Figure 4.3b.

As shown in Figure 4.3 that the proposed NDNN consists of L layers (where $L = 4$) with K hidden units in each layer. The output of each layer is forwarded as an input to the next consecutive layer in the training process. Assuming that Y_L is representing the output of

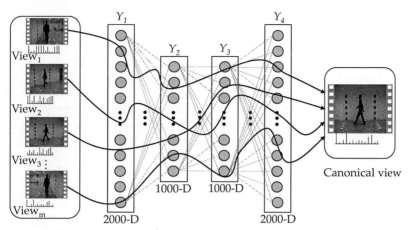

(a) The mapping/transformation from source viewpoints to the canonical view.

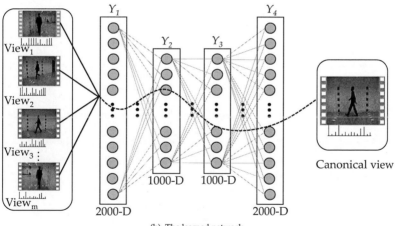

(b) The learned network.

Figure 4.3: The proposed NDNN. (a) Training process: for m different source viewpoints there are m different virtual paths connecting them to the canonical view. (b) The learned network: it forces the m different virtual paths to learn a single, high-level and shared virtual path (dotted line) which connects all the source viewpoints to the canonical view.

L-th layer and $X_{ij} \in \mathbb{R}$ is the j-th training instance obtained from i-th viewpoint, the output of the first layer is computed as [Kha+18b],

$$Y_1 = f(W_1 X_{ij} + b_1), \tag{4.1}$$

where Y_1 represents the output of first layer and $f(\cdot)$ is the non-linear activation function. Moreover, W_1 and b_1 are respectively the weight matrix and bias vector to be learned for the first layer. Usually, the activation function which includes hyperbolic tangent function $\tanh(x)$, the logistic function $f(x) = \frac{1}{(1+e^{-x})}$, and the Rectified Linear Unit (ReLU) $f(x) = \max(0, x)$ are used in neural networks. However, the proposed network employs Leaky Rectified Linear Unit (leakyReLU) as an activation function. It is a variant of ReLU, perform efficiently and unlike other activation functions such as sigmoid it does not suffer from vanishing gradient problem [Kha+18b]. In comparison with ReLU, it permits a small non-zero gradient when the unit is saturated and not active [MHN13]. In particular, it assigns a small slope to the negative part rather than completely dropping it. Mathematically, it can be written as,

$$f(x) = \begin{cases} x & \text{if } x > 0; \\ \alpha x & \text{otherwise} \end{cases} \tag{4.2}$$

where α is a small constant. The output of the first layer Y_1 is forwarded as an input to the second layer which would be processed as,

$$Y_2 = f(W_2 Y_1 + b_2), \tag{4.3}$$

where Y_2 represents the output of the second layer, W_2 and b_2 are respectively the weight matrix and the bias vector to be learned for the second layer. The output of the last fully connected layer is computed as [Kha+18b],

$$t(X_{ij}) = Y_L = f(W_L Y_{L-1} + b_L), \tag{4.4}$$

where Y_L is the output of the last layer and $t(X_{ij})$ represents the non-linear transformation function determined by the parameters W_L and b_L. During the training, the input and output to the proposed NDNN are the spatiotemporal gait descriptors from the source and canonical viewpoints, respectively. Recall that the proposed algorithm exploits the spatiotemporal gait descriptors of gait sequences from the side-view walk as canonical view. Therefore, the proposed network tries to get the output of $t(X_{ij})$ to be close to the respective canonical view X_{cj} (*i.e.*, $t(X_{ij}) \approx X_{cj}$; where X_{cj} is representing the corresponding j-th training instance from canonical viewpoint), regardless of its input view as described earlier.

Furthermore, the proposed network do not require the information of viewpoints and other variations in the gait during the training of network, and similarly at the construction of cross-view gait descriptors. To efficiently learn the underlying structure of the data, the size of the network (*i.e.*, the number of layers and the hidden units in each layer) is chosen empirically. Due to the length of spatiotemporal gait descriptors, the size of the first and the last layers are set to $2,000$ whereas, the size of two intermediate layers is set to $1,000$ for each. The first two layers of the network eliminate the redundant information in the input descriptors by mapping it to a high-level but low-dimensional representation. Afterward, this low-dimensional compact representation is mapped back to a high-dimensional output layer using the last two connected layers as demonstrated in Figure 4.3b. The output of the last layer delivers the canonical representation of the input descriptors.

The learning of the proposed NDNN consists of minimizing the loss function of the reconstruction error over all training samples from all viewpoints by updating the set of parameters $\Theta = \{W_L, b_L | L = 1, 2, \ldots, 4\}$. Moreover, weight decay J_w is added to penalize the objective function, in order to reduce the effect of over-fitting. Large weights may cause highly curved and non-smooth mappings [Ben12]. The weight decay penalizes the large weights and keeps them small to make the mappings smooth and to reduce the over-fitting [Kha+18b]. Assuming that there are m different viewpoints and n instances in each view, the following loss function of the reconstruction error e_Θ is minimized:

$$e_\Theta = \frac{1}{mn} \sum_{i-1}^{m} \sum_{j-1}^{n} \| X_{cj} - t(X_{ij}) \|^2 + \lambda J_w, \tag{4.5}$$

where $i = 1, \ldots, m$ are the viewpoints, $j = 1, \ldots, n$ are the training instances and c is the canonical view. Moreover, λ represents the weight decay parameter and $J_w = \sum_{k=1}^{K} W_k^2$ is L_2 regularization. The proposed NDNN employs mini-batch stochastic gradient descent method through back-propagation to minimize the loss function e_Θ over all training samples.

4.3 Cross-view Gait Representation and Classification

It can be observed in Equation 4.4 that $t(X_{ij})$ is a non-linear transformation function which transform the gait sequence X_{ij} to its respective canonical view X_{cj}. In particular, this function provides the canonical view representation of gait sequences obtained from any unknown viewpoint, which can be used as cross-view gait representation. Since the proposed NDNN consists of a set of non-linear transformations $\{Y_1, \ldots, Y_4\}$ to map the gait sequences from

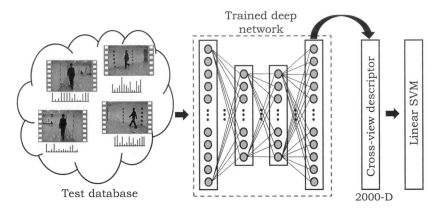

Figure 4.4: An example depicting the construction of cross-view descriptors and their classification. The output of last layer is used as cross-view gait descriptor.

different viewpoints to a canonical view, the output of the last layer in the proposed NDNN is selected as cross-view gait descriptor (Figure 4.4) because it encodes the influence of all these transformations and provides the canonical-view representation of gait regardless of its input view. Assuming that $X'_{ij} \in \mathbb{R}$ is the j-th testing instance from any unknown i-th viewpoint, the formulation of its final cross-view gait descriptor can be described as,

$$t(X'_{ij}) = f(W_L \dots f(W_2(f(W_1 X'_{ij} + b_1)) + b_2) + \dots + b_L) \tag{4.6}$$

where $t(X'_{ij}) \approx X'_{cj}$. The obtained cross-view gait representation certainly comprises the impact of all non-linear transformations from i-th viewpoint to canonical view. To perform cross-view gait recognition, the gait descriptors from the gallery set are selected and their cross-view gait representation is obtained using the learned NDNN (*i.e.*, by propagating them through the trained network). These cross-view descriptors along with their respective labels are used to train a classifier. The proposed technique employs a simple linear SVM [Fan+08a] to demonstrate the robustness of proposed NDNN. For a testing instance, its cross-view gait representation is obtained using the Equation 4.6 and fed to SVM to recognise an individual.

4.4 Experiments and Results

The experimental evaluation is carried out on two large benchmark cross-view gait databases: CASIA-B [Yu+06] and OULP [Iwa+12], to demonstrate the effectiveness of the

Table 4.1: Summary of the cross-view gait databases used in performance evaluation. Views represent the number of viewpoints which are used in the database recording and size is the number of gait video sequences in each view which are used in experimental evaluation.

Database	Views	Size	Walk Scenarios
CASIA-B	11	1,240	Normal walk, walk with bag, walk with coat
OULP	4	≈ 3,700	Normal walk

proposed cross-view gait recognition algorithm. The summary of both cross-view gait databases is presented in Table 4.1. Several experiments are performed on each of the databases and their recognition accuracies are compared with the existing state-of-the-art techniques.

Implementation detail

As mentioned earlier, the proposed cross-view gait recognition algorithm employs the gait representation technique presented in Chapter 3. In particular, the spatiotemporal based gait descriptors are obtained for all the video sequences from each viewpoint. To construct a deep neural network, an open source library Keras [Cho+15] with Tensorflow [Aba+16] at backend is used. During the training, the input to the proposed NDNN are the spatiotemporal gait descriptors of individuals from all possible different viewpoints and the output are the spatiotemporal gait descriptors from the respective canonical view. The gait sequences recorded from a lateral viewpoint (*i.e.*, 90°) are used as canonical view representation. The first step in the training of proposed NDNN is the initialization of network parameter $\Theta = \{W_L, b_L | \ L = 1,2,...,4\}$. Due to small number of layers, the network parameters are initialized using simple random initialization method [Ben12]. Specifically, the weight matrix W_L is initialized using a Gaussian distribution with zero mean and 0.05 standard deviation and all the bias terms b_L are initialized with zero.

The network is trained using a variant of gradient descent-based method known as RMSprop [TH12] with its default parameters (*e.g.* learning rate is initialized with 0.001), for 150 epochs. Instead of using a fixed learning rate for each parameter, RMSprop uses a different learning rate for each parameter and they are adaptive. That is, the learning rate are updated by the exponentially decaying average of squared gradients obtained in the previous iterations. Mini-batch gradient descent method is used to update the weights in order to minimize the error of the model on the training dataset. That is, small batches of the training dataset are used to calculate the model error and update the model parameters during the training. The size of the mini-batch is set to 64. The proposed NDNN exploits leakyReLU as a non-linear activation function with α is set to 0.01. The network consists of 4 layers and the training process is carried out using back-propagation with regression loss defined by the Equation 4.5. The weight decay parameter is set to 0.0001.

It can be observed that the proposed NDNN consists of several hyper-parameters such as number of layers, layer sizes, activation function, learning rate, etc. The tuning process of these parameters is more empirical than theoretical. For all these hyper-parameters of NDNN, a multi-resolution search [Ben12] is exploited in order to obtain their optimal values. That is, first the parameter-values are evaluated within a larger range and few best configurations are selected. Later, a narrow search space is exploited in the second step around these values to select the optimal one. For example, by following [Lar+07], the performance of the proposed NDNN is evaluated with the increasing number of hidden layers until it obtained a peak performance on the validation dataset. It is empirically concluded that the performance of the proposed network did not further improve by increasing the number of hidden layers beyond two. Similarly, the sizes of each hidden layer (*i.e.*, hidden units) are evaluated in the range [500,1500]. In particular, the network is trained several times with different values of hyper-parameters in order to learn a good architecture. Following the aforementioned proposed architecture, first the network is trained using a gradient descent based algorithm. In the second step, the gait sequences from gallery and probe datasets are propagated over the trained network and their canonical-view (*i.e.*, cross-view) gait representation is obtained. Recall, the output of the last layer in the network is used as cross-view gait representation, therefore they are 2,000 dimensional long descriptors. Finally, the obtained gait descriptors are classified using a subsequent classifier to recognize the identity of the walker in a cross-view environment. It uses a simple linear SVM as classifier to demonstrate the effectiveness of the proposed network and discriminative nature of the descriptors. The experimental evaluation is carried out on a machine with an Intel i7-6700K CPU, 64GB RAM and a NVidia GTX TITAN X GPU.

Performance evaluation on CASIA-B dataset

The CASIA-B database comprises the gait sequences of 124 subjects. The database is recorded in an indoor environment using eleven different viewing angles: $0°, 18°, 36°, \ldots, 180°$. Figure 4.5 presents a sample image from each viewpoint to demonstrate the variations in appearance due to change in the viewing angle. Each subject in the database has ten video sequences of gait recorded from each viewpoint with three different variations, namely: normal walk (*nm*), walk with bag (*bg*), and walk with coat (*cl*). There are six sequences of *nm* and two sequences to each *bg* and *cl*. CASIA-B is a large cross-view gait database and the gait recognition on this database under different viewpoints is challenging, particularly

Figure 4.5: Example images of CASIA-B database from each viewpoint 0° to 180° (left to right).

when the cross-view angle is large. It is even more difficult when the probe and gallery sets belong to different walking scenarios [Wu+17; PP+16]. For example, the gallery set consists of normal walk sequences and the probe set comprises the walk sequences with coat from a different viewpoint.

Similar to [Wu+17], the database is divided into two parts. The first part which comprises the randomly selected gait sequences of 24 subjects (in total 5,280 gait sequences) are used to train the proposed NDNN. The viewpoint 90° is selected as a canonical view. The second part which comprises the gait sequences of remaining 100 subjects are used to evaluate the performance of proposed cross-view gait recognition algorithm. In particular, the second part is used to construct a gallery and probe sets. For all experiments, the first four sequences of normal walk (i.e., $nm_1 - nm_4$) from 100 subjects are used to from a gallery set and the rest are used in different probe sets. The proposed algorithm has performed three different types of experiments, as designed by the most recent state-of-the-art techniques [PP+16; Wu+17; Tan+17]. In the first set of experiments, the gallery set (V_g) comprises the gait sequences from multiple viewpoints excluding the identical view which is placed in the probe set (V_p). The recognition accuracies achieved by the proposed algorithm and their comparisons with existing techniques are reported in Table 4.2. The statistics demonstrate that the proposed algorithm outperforms the compared methods in all the experiments with significant margin.

In the second set of experiments, similar to [Zha+17; LLT11] the gallery set (V_g) consists of the gait sequences from viewing angle 90° and the gait sequences from the rest of the viewpoints are used in probe sets (V_p), separately. Table 4.3 presents the recognition accu-

Table 4.2: Comparison of recognition accuracies (%) on CASIA-B gait database. The gallery set (V_g) contains the gait sequences from all views except the identical view in the probe set (V_p). The best results are marked in bold. Note that hyphen (-) means that either the results are not available or the respective approach cannot be evaluated under those experiments.

$V_g : nm_1 - nm_4$	0° - 180°				36° - 144°		
$V_p : nm_5 - nm_6$	0°	54°	90°	126°	54°	90°	126°
SVR [Kus+10]	-	28	29	34	35	44	45
TSVD [Kus+09b]	-	39	33	42	49	50	54
CMCC [Kus+14]	46.3	52.4	48.3	56.9	-	-	-
ViDP [Hu+13b]	-	59.1	50.2	57.5	83.5	76.7	80.7
CNN [Wu+17]	54.8	77.8	64.9	76.1	90.8	85.8	90.4
Proposed NDNN	**58.5**	**97.5**	**91.5**	**97.0**	**98.5**	**93.5**	**98.0**

racies achieved by the proposed algorithm and their comparison with existing techniques. The results show that the proposed algorithm outperforms the existing methods in all experiments except viewing angle 72°, where GII [Zha+17] performs better than the proposed technique. It is worth mentioning that unlike GII [Zha+17] which learns a separate mapping for each subject with the rest in view-pairs, the proposed NDNN learns a single model for

Table 4.3: Comparison of recognition accuracies (%) on CASIA-B gait database with gallery view V_g is 90°. The best results are marked in bold. Note that hyphen (-) means that either the results are not available or the respective approach cannot be evaluated under those experiments.

$V_p : nm_5 - nm_6$	0°	18°	36°	54°	72°	108°	126°	144°	162°	180°
JDLDA [PP+16]	20	25	37	58	94	-	-	-	-	-
Method [Kus+12a]	12	20	30	60	92	92	62	35	19	12
MvDA [Man+14a]	17	27	36	64	95	-	-	-	-	-
GII [Zha+17]	17	26	54	84	**98**	98	84	50	25	14
JSL [LLT11]	20.5	35.5	56.5	81.5	96.5	96	89.5	50	34.5	21.5
DATER [Hu13]	3.2	7.4	16.8	48.1	66.5	-	-	-	-	-
Method [Kus+14]	18	24	41	66	96	95	68	41	21	13
Method [Zhe+11]	-	-	-	42	86	88	50	26	-	-
Proposed NDNN	**75**	**74.5**	**78**	**88.5**	97	**98.5**	**91.5**	**75.5**	**74.5**	**75.5**

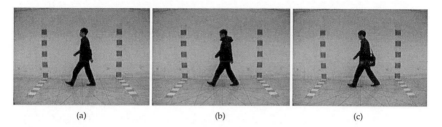

(a) (b) (c)

Figure 4.6: Sample images from CASIA-B dataset demonstrating the variations in walk. (a) Normal walk, (b) walk with coat, and (c) walk with bag.

all the subjects to map their gait sequences from all possible multiple viewpoints to a single canonical view.

To verify the robustness of the proposed algorithm, it is also evaluated under various conditions of walk in this database. Figure 4.6 presents few sample images from the database illustrating three variations of walk recorded from viewing angle 90°. In the last set of experiments, the same distribution of gait sequences is adopted as stated in [Tan+17]. The gallery set comprises the gait sequences of normal walk from viewing angle 36° to 144°, and the probe set comprises the gait sequences under various conditions recorded at 54°, 90° and 126° separately. Table 4.4 presents the recognition accuracies achieved by the proposed algorithm and their comparison with existing techniques. The statistics show that the proposed algorithm outperforms the compared methods in most experiments.

Table 4.4: Comparison of recognition accuracies (%) on CASIA-B gait database under various walking conditions. In each block, two recognition results of bg and cl are presented with the separation of '/'. The best results are marked in bold.

V_p	54° (bg/cl)	90° (bg/cl)	126° (bg/cl)
Method [Tan+17]	94.2 / 93.5	**92.3 / 92.0**	95.1 / **94.2**
Method [RJM16]	76.4 / 87.9	73.7 / 91.1	76.9 / 86.2
RLTDA [Hu13]	80.8 / 69.4	76.5 / 72.1	72.3 / 64.4
R-VTM [Zhe+11]	40.7 / 35.4	58.2 / 50.3	59.4 / 61.3
FT-SVD [Mak+06]	26.5 / 19.8	33.1 / 20.6	38.6 / 32.0
CNN [Wu+17]	92.7 / 49.7	88.9 / 75.6	86.0 / 51.4
Proposed NDNN	**96.0 / 94.5**	87.5 / 91.0	**98.5 / 94.2**

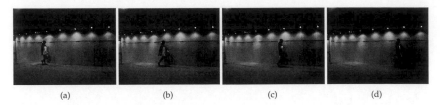

(a)   (b)   (c)   (d)

Figure 4.7: Sample images from OULP gait dataset. (a) 55°, (b) 65°, (c) 75°, and (d) 85°.

Performance evaluation on OULP dataset

The OU-ISIR large population (OULP) is one of the largest cross-view gait database, recorded in an indoor environment at 30 f/s. The database consists of the gait sequences from more than 4,000 subjects and they are recorded under four viewing angles: 55°,65°,75° and 85°. Each subject in the database was asked to walk along a course twice in a natural manner (*i.e.*, normal walk). Few sample images of a walking subject in the database from each viewpoint are shown in Figure 4.7. Similar to most recent techniques [Li+17; Shi+16; Che+17b], two distinct type of experiments are performed on this database: same-view experiments and cross-view experiments. In the same-view experimental setting, the gallery and the probe gait sequences belong to same viewpoint, whereas in cross-view experimental setting they belong to different viewpoints. Specifically, the proposed technique build a gallery set by picking the gait sequences from each view iteratively (*i.e.*, from {55°,65°,75°,85°}) and place the gait sequences from the rest of the three views in probe set separately. The viewpoint 85° is selected as a canonical view.

The authors in [Iwa+12] have defined the distribution of OULP database into five parts which were made publicly available [1]. Each part comprises the division of gait sequences from 1,912 subjects in two equivalent disjoint sets. Similar to [Li+17; Shi+16; Che+17b; Wu+17; MMY16], the proposed technique has performed a five 2-fold cross validations in both type of experiments to meet the protocol of benchmark. In particular, a 2-fold cross validation is adopted for each part when the training and testing sets are exchanged, and this process is carried out for all of the five parts. In each part, one set is used to train the proposed NDNN and the other is exploited for testing purpose (*i.e.*, to construct the gallery and probe sets), and vice versa. Table 4.5 presents the average recognition accuracies achieved by the proposed algorithm and their comparison with existing techniques. The results demonstrate that the proposed technique outperforms the existing methods in most experiments.

---

[1] http://www.am.sanken.osaka-u.ac.jp/BiometricDB/dataset/GaitLP/Benchmarks.html

Table 4.5: Performance evaluation (%) and comparison of recognition accuracies with the existing methods on OULP gait database under same-view and cross-view experiments. The recognition results in same-view experiments are reported in parenthesis (). The best results are marked in bold. Note that hyphen (-) means that either the results are not available or the respective approach cannot be evaluated under those experiments.

Gallery	Method	Probe			
		55°	65°	75°	85°
	DeepGait [Li+17]	(97.4)	96.1	93.4	88.7
	wQVTM [MMY16]	-	78.3	64.0	48.6
	GEINet [Shi+16]	(94.7)	93.2	89.7	79.9
	Method [Che+17b]	(95.2)	93.6	81.2	62.2
55°	PdVS [Mur+15]	-	76.2	61.4	45.5
	AVTM [Mur+15]	-	77.7	64.5	42.7
	Method [Wu+17]	(98.8)	**98.3**	**96.0**	80.5
	Proposed NDNN	**(100)**	95.1	94.9	**97.5**
	DeepGait [Li+17]	**97.3**	(97.6)	97.2	95.4
	wQVTM [MMY16]	81.5	-	79.2	67.5
	GEINet [Shi+16]	93.7	(95.1)	93.8	90.6
	Method [Che+17b]	90.9	(95.3)	95.5	90.2
65°	PdVS [Mur+15]	76	-	77.1	65.5
	AVTM [Mur+15]	75.6	-	76.4	62.8
	Method [Wu+17]	96.3	(98.9)	**97.3**	83.3
	Proposed NDNN	94.8	**(100)**	95.5	**97.5**
	DeepGait [Li+17]	93.3	97.5	(97.7)	97.6
	wQVTM [MMY16]	70.2	80.0	-	78.2
	GEINet [Shi+16]	90.1	94.1	(95.2)	93.8
	Method [Che+17b]	77.5	94.4	(96.0)	96.0
75°	PdVS [Mur+15]	60.3	76.2	-	76.5
	AVTM [Mur+15]	59.9	74.9	-	76.3
	Method [Wu+17]	94.2	**97.8**	(98.9)	85.1
	Proposed NDNN	**95.1**	96.0	**(100)**	**97.7**
	DeepGait [Li+17]	89.3	96.4	98.3	(98.3)
	wQVTM [MMY16]	51.1	68.5	79.0	-
	GEINet [Shi+16]	81.4	91.2	94.6	(94.7)
	Method [Che+17b]	55.4	87.1	94.8	(94.7)
85°	PdVS [Mur+15]	40.5	60.6	73.1	-
	AVTM [Mur+15]	40.2	61.9	74.3	-
	Method [Wu+17]	90.0	96.0	**98.4**	(98.9)
	Proposed NDNN	**98.0**	**97.1**	97.7	**(100)**

The recognition accuracies reported in Table 4.2– 4.5 demonstrate that the proposed algorithm perform better than state-of-the-art cross-view gait recognition techniques in numerous experiments. Moreover, along with cross-view variations the proposed NDNN has been proven to be robust against variations in clothing and carrying a bag during the walk. The superior performance of the proposed technique is based on two factors: An efficient gait representation, and an effective non-linear view transformation model. The spatiotemporal based gait representation is computed directly from the video sequences which encodes the person static appearance and motion information. The proposed NDNN is capable to capture the non-linear manifolds in gait sequences and learns a multi-step virtual path between the different source viewpoints and their respective canonical view. Due to these advantages, the proposed technique has achieved higher cross-view gait recognition results than the existing methods.

4.5   Summary

This chapter introduced a cross-view gait recognition technique using the spatiotemporal gait representation. First, the spatiotemporal gait descriptors are directly computed from the video sequences, as described in Chapter 3. Second, a non-linear VTM is introduced in Section 4.2 that learns a single model to map the gait sequences from multiple different viewpoints to a single canonical view. Finally, the construction of cross-view gait descriptors using the learned model and their classification is presented in Section 4.3. The experimental evaluation is carried out on two large cross-view bench mark gait databases and their recognition results are discussed in Section 4.4.

Chapter 5

Movement Analysis of Human Body Parts

Movement analysis of human body parts plays a vital role in several applications *e.g.* clinical diagnostics and assessment systems, sports-based systems to analyze the performance of athletes, the analysis of human activities in daily life. In this chapter, a computer vision-based method is introduced to analyze the movements of different human body parts for clinical diagnosis. The proposed method detects different human body parts in videos and tracks them temporally without using markers or wearable sensors. The aim of the proposed method is to assist the clinicians and general practitioners in the early detection of movement disorders in infants. Most existing techniques use markers [Mei+06; Hon+13] or wearable sensors [PLC05; Hei+10] to detect and track the body parts with the help of visual sensors. Such techniques are suitable for adults, however it is not an effective solution for infants because they might feel discomforted by wearing such sensors [Kha+16b] and this can affect their natural movements.

This chapter proposed a framework to detect the movements disorders (*e.g.* cerebral palsy) in infants. Such disorders may appear due to genetic disorders or the abnormalities in the infant's brain during the pregnancy or at birth. The analysis of such movement disorders in the early stage is very important for the early intervention and setting up a treatment program to follow-up [Gro+05; Pie02; Mei+06; Sta+12]. Generally, the doctors and the physiotherapists use GMA [Pre01; Gro+05] method to detect the movement disorders which analyzes the spontaneous movements of different body parts. However, it is a tedious activity to manually observe the movements of every infant. Additionally, it is a subjective procedure and the outcomes are based on the observer's expertise. To conquer these limitations, an automatic vision-based system is proposed to accurately analyze the movements of infant's body parts.

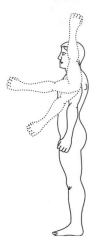

Figure 5.1: An example image illustrating the large articulation in the human arm [CHE15].

5.1   A Deformable Part-based Model for Movement Analysis of Infants

An automatic detection of body parts in an image is a challenging task due to the variations in their appearances because of colours, shapes, sizes, occlusions and others. Moreover, the human body has many degrees of freedom in the articulation of body parts which may result in extensive variations in the appearance. For example, Figure 5.1 presents such appearance-changes in the human arm.

The proposed body parts detection technique is based on the principle of pictorial structure framework [FE73; Fel+10; YR13] which states that an object's appearance can be represented using a collection of part-templates together with the spatial relations between the parts. That is, the human body structure is detected in the proposed technique using the part-templates (*i.e.*, part-filters) along with the spatial relations between the parts. In particular, the proposed method begins by detecting the different body parts which are based on joint locations, and computes angles at predicted joints. Later, the movement at different joints is encoded by tracking the orientations in the temporal direction. To automatically detect the body parts, the proposed technique learned a model from a set of training images to prepare the part-filters and the spatial relations between the parts. To cope with the problem of appearance changes due to large articulation in body parts (Figure 5.1), their appearance changes are encoded using the mixture of part-filters and the spatial relation

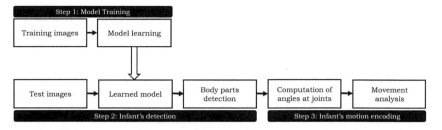

Figure 5.2: An overview of the proposed framework for movement analysis.

between the involved parts. The model is represented using tree-structured graphs and the learning process is carried out using the Structured Support Vector Machine (structSVM).

The proposed technique operates in three steps. In the first step, a model is learned to detect the skeleton information of infant which comprises the set of part-filters and the spatial relations between them. In the second step, the body parts are detected in the test images using the learned model. Finally, the angles are computed at predicted joint locations and their orientation is tracked in the successive frames to encode the movements. A block diagram representing the entire process is illustrated in Figure 5.2. The detailed description of each step in the proposed technique is outlined in the subsequent sections. However, the detection step is explained prior to the model's training in order to enhance the readability.

5.2 Template-based Model for Infant's Detection

As mentioned earlier that the learned model consists of a mixture of part-filters build for each body part and the spatial relations between the parts. However, each filter in the same mixture corresponds to a different orientation of the part, known as the *state* of the part. In a given test image, the body parts are detected by applying these filters to convolute over a HOG of the image. For the first frame in a video, the detection process exploits all locations and scales of the image and a score of each part-filter is computed which reveals the likelihood of occurrence of a particular state. This exhaustive search is performed only once for the first frame of the video. Since the camera was fixed during the recording and infants are not making any rapid movements (*i.e.*, changing their place), the predicted location of infant in previous frame with the relaxation of a certain threshold pixel (Ω_{dist}) in all directions is employed to set the search-space in the succeeding frame. This search-space optimization is not only helpful in improving the detection accuracy but also decreases the computation cost.

Assuming that $f_{p_a}^{s_a}$ is a part-filter (or template) of size $M \times N$ defined for the body part p_a, where $a \in \{1, \ldots, K\}$. Moreover, $s_a \in \{1, \ldots, S\}$ represents the set of states for part p_a and FR is the response (i.e., score) of a part-filter in HOG image I_Φ at location $l = I_\Phi(x, y)$. This score can be computed by matching the $f_{p_a}^{s_a}$ with the patch of I_Φ as described in the following,

$$FR(f_{p_a}^{s_a}, I_\Phi, l) = \sum_{m=1}^{M} \sum_{n=1}^{N} f_{p_a}^{s_a}(m, n) I_\Phi(x + m, y + n), \tag{5.1}$$

where $f_{p_a}^{s_a}(m, n)$ represents a pixel location in the filter. Equation 5.1 is indeed a cross-correlation [Kha+16c] which measures the similarity score between $f_{p_a}^{s_a}$ and the patch of I_Φ at location l. The score is computed at each location of I_Φ, and the highest scoring value represents the best matching location of respective part-filter. The part-filter scores are computed in multi-scale fashion, however the proposed algorithm is described here considering the full-scale image to keep the discussion simple.

To encode the spatial relations between body parts, the proposed model is represented using a tree-structured graph $G = (V, E)$, where V is the set of vertices representing the body parts and E are the edges to define the relations between them. Furthermore, the articulation between the parts is modeled using a set of springs [YR13] which encode a spatial relation between a part and its parent-part, e.g. hand and elbow. For example, if a part has 5 different states and its parent also exhibits 5 different states, then there are 25 springs which characterize the relative placement of a child and its parent body part by applying all combinations of springs hence, demonstrating 25 different orientations. That is, each spring is tailored for a specific combination of parent's and child's state. Assuming that p_a and p_b are respectively representing the body-part and its parent-part, the score for the detection of a part and its state can be defined as,

$$Score(I, l, s) = \sum_{a \in V} f_{p_a}^{s_a}(I_\Phi, l_a) + D(p_a, p_b) + CO(s) \tag{5.2}$$

Equation 5.2 consists of three terms. The first term computes the response of a part-filter $f_{p_a}^{s_a}$ in I_Φ at location l_a. The second term D defines a spring model between part p_a and p_b using the distance information between them and can be formulated as [Kha+18c],

$$D(p_a, p_b) = \sum_{a, b \in E} \zeta_{p_a, p_b}^{s_a, s_b} \Psi(l_a - l_b), \tag{5.3}$$

where $\zeta_{p_a, p_b}^{s_a, s_b}$ is a deformation parameter which encodes the placement of a part relative to its rest location; i.e., the relative location of p_a to its parent p_b based on their states s_a and s_b, respectively. Moreover, $\Psi(l_a - l_b) = [d_x, d_y, d_x^2, d_y^2]$ represents the predicted relative displacement of p_a with respect to p_b in terms of pixel grid, where $d_x = x_a - x_b$ and $d_y = y_a - y_b$. Equation 5.3 computes the deformation cost using a particular combination of states which describe the difference between the predicted and presumed relative position of a part to its parent in xy coordinates. In particular, it penalized the score based on the the deviation of predicted location from rest location. The third term in Equation 5.2 describes the co-occurrences of part's states and can be written as [YR13],

$$CO(s) = \sum_{a \in V} R_{p_a}^{s_a} + \sum_{a,b \in E} R_{p_a,p_b}^{s_a,s_b}, \tag{5.4}$$

where the first term in Equation 5.4 is $R_{p_a}^{s_a}$ which describes the assignment of one particular state for part p_a, while the pairwise feature $R_{p_a,p_b}^{s_a,s_b}$ represents a trained co-occurrence between the parts p_a and p_b using their states s_a and s_b. As mentioned earlier that the proposed method employs a tree-structured graph G to encode that which parts of the model have logical relations. It rewards a positive score to the parts having a logical relation, and a negative score to the illogical relations.

It can be observed from Equation 5.2 that the final score is computed by the sum of local scores for all possible states which is modified by the deformation and co-occurrence constraints of the parts. These modifications are based on their deviation from the trained model. Using this formulation, the aim is to maximize the score over locations l and states s. Assuming that z_a is represent the pixel location and state of part p_a, i.e., $z_a = (l_a, s_a)$ and $C\{a\}$ is children of part p_a. The score of part p_a is computed as:

$$S_{p_a}(z_a) = FR(f_{p_a}^{s_a}, I_\Phi, l_a) + R_{p_a}^{s_a} + \sum_{\acute{a} \in C\{a\}} Score_{\acute{a}}(z_a) \tag{5.5}$$

The proposed method computes the local score of part p_a at all pixel location l_a for all possible state s_a by collecting the score of its children using Equation 5.2. The overall score which is passes to parent part p_b is computed as,

$$S_b(z_b) = \max_{z_a} \left[S_{p_a}(z_a) + D(p_a, p_b) + R_{p_a,p_b}^{s_a,s_b} \right] \tag{5.6}$$

Equation 5.6 is computed for part p_b which seeks the best scoring location and state of its child-part p_a. To search different body parts efficiently, the proposed method employs the concept of independence assumption. For example in a given torso rather than using many cascade loops to detect all the other parts, the proposed method searches independently the best candidates of arms, legs and so forth. Since a tree-structured graph is used to encode the spatial relations between the parts, it can be achieved efficiently using dynamic programming [Fel+10]. In particular, the detection process of the proposed method iterates over all the body parts, computes the score starting from the leaf-node (*i.e.*, feet) and passes to their respective parent which ultimately ends at the root-node (*i.e.*, head) as described in Equation 5.5– 5.6. Hence, the high scoring root location determine the detection of body-model. However, it may introduce many overlapping detections in one image. Since the proposed method is designed for infant's detection and the recorded data consists of only one subject in an image, non-maximum suppression is employed to greedily pick the highest scoring location as an estimation. Moreover, the proposed detection process also saves the *argmax* indices in Equation 5.6 which reflects the locations of the selected parts. Therefore, the highest scoring body-model can be recreated directly using the root location only. Nonetheless, the self occlusion of body parts which is a common scenario in case of infant's movement misleads the detection process and may introduce false alarms. To conquer this issue, the proposed method also saves the detection score of each part while saving their locations in Equation 5.6. At reconstruction stage, it iterates over each individual part and compare their scores with a pre-defined threshold Ω_{score}, rather than picking the high-scoring root configuration of parts. The maximum scoring location of each part which should also satisfy the Ω_{score} is chosen as the correct part.

5.3   Infant's Motion Analysis

The proposed method exploits angle orientations at different joints and their tracking in the temporal direction to encode the infant's motion information. Since the body parts are located at joints, the proposed method computes the skeleton information at predicted joint locations. In particular, the angles are computed at joints such as elbow, shoulder, knee, *etc.* and their tracking in successive frames of a video prompts the movement of the respective parts. In order to compute the angle, consider a case of the knee joint which is connected with the ankle and hip. Assuming that l_i, l_j and l_k are representing the predicted ankle, knee and hip joints respectively (Figure 5.3). The proposed method computes two vectors V_1 and V_2 as described in the following,

$$V_1 = l_i - l_j$$
$$V_2 = l_k - l_j$$
(5.7)

The angle θ is computed between V_1 and V_2 using a following simple cosine equation which represents the angle orientation at the knee joint,

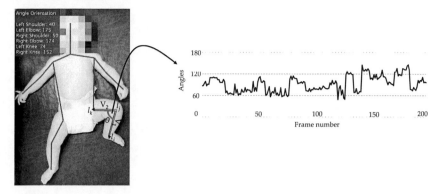

Figure 5.3: An example of angle computation at left knee and its tracking in successive 200 frames. The angle orientations at other joints are annotated at the upper-left corner of the test image.

$$\theta = arccos\left(\frac{V_1 \cdot V_2}{|V_1||V_2|}\right) \tag{5.8}$$

Analogously, the angles are computed for other joints as annotated at the upper-left corner of the test image (Figure 5.3). The tracking of these angle orientations across the successive frames in a video sequence is used to encode the movements at a particular joint. Figure 5.3 demonstrates the movements using the angle orientations in the left knee of an infant from the 200 successive frames in a video.

5.4 Model Training

The proposed method uses a set of positive images annotated with marked body parts locations and a set of negative images without any infant to train a model. Each positive image in the training dataset requires 14 annotated parts which are located at joint locations. Figure 5.4 illustrates the marked points on the infant's body region. All the positive images are scaled, flipped and rotated by a few degree to make the model robust and scale-invariant. In particular, the positive images in the training dataset are rotated between -15° to +15° with an interval of 5°, and horizontally flipped. The proposed model manually defines the edge relations E in a tree-structured graph by connecting the joint locations. To define the dimensions of a bounding-box around the part, first the length of each body part is computed from a set of positive images. Later, the ratio between the length of each part in

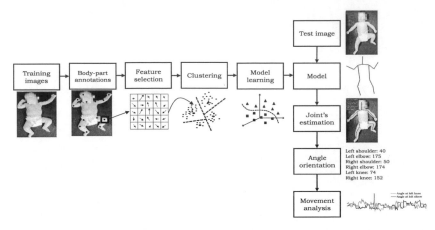

Figure 5.4: An illustration of model training, and the detection and the tracking of body parts.

an image to the median value of the length of that part in a complete training set is used to set the dimensions of bounding-box for all the parts in that image. All those bounding-boxes having dimensions less than 30×30 pixels are discarded in the training process. The proposed algorithm computes features on these annotated locations to describe their appearances. In particular, it computes orientation of edges at each joint within the patch of 40×40 pixels, saved them using the quantization of their orientation information into 8-bin histogram and normalized with L_2-norm. The orientation information is saved in 5×5 cells. One can observe several variations in the appearance of the human body parts due to many degrees of freedom in the articulation of body parts, as depicted in Figure 5.1. In order to cope this problem, several filters are created for each body part to encode their all possible orientations. Specifically, the appearances of each body part is grouped into several clusters based on their orientations in the training images. Since it can be observed that the appearance changes in several parts (*i.e.*, state) are based on their relative location from their respective parent part. Therefore, in order to define the all possible states of a part, their relative locations in the set of positive images are grouped into S clusters using k-means clustering algorithm. That is, each cluster represents a unique state of the part. Since all the body parts do not possess the similar degrees of articulation, the cluster size is not fixed for all the parts to define their states. It can vary based on the degree of articulation at particular part *e.g.* the arms and legs parts comprise more articulation in comparison with the torso.

The aim of the model training is to obtain a set of part-filters for each body part and the spatial relations between them such that the model can discriminate between positive examples and negative examples by assigning a high positive score to the parts in the positive image and a low score to the parts in the negative image. Specifically, for a given training set of positive images { $I_{pos}, l_{pos}, s_{pos}$ } and negative images { I_{neg}} the problem of learning the model parameters consists of finding a set of part-filters and deformation parameters which are computed using the structured prediction objective function proposed in [Fel+10]. Assuming that $z_n = (l_n, s_n)$, then using Equation 5.2 it can be defined as $S(I, z) = \beta.(I_\Phi, z)$. It can be observed in Equation 5.2 that score is linear in a part-filter matching (*i.e.*, similarity score) and deformation cost (*i.e.*, the dot product of two vectors results in a scalar). Therefore, all the HOG features of body parts and theirs rest location information is concatenated into one big vector (I_Φ, z) and their dot product is obtained with the local templates and spring parameters β. Ideally, this computation should produce a positive score for the locations in positive image and a negative score for all the locations in negative image. In other words, these parameters should satisfy the following constraints:

$$\beta \cdot (I_{pos}, z) \geq +1 \quad \forall I_{pos}$$
$$\beta \cdot (I_{neg}, z) \leq -1 \quad \forall I_{neg}$$

$$(5.9)$$

The above constraints show that the parameter β should be capable to discriminate between positive examples and negative examples by assigning them a positive and negative score, respectively. Therefore, based on such an explicit formulation a simple SVM based classifier can be used to learn the value of the parameters (*i.e.*, β). SVM maps the training instances into high dimensional space and extracts a decision boundary (*e.g.* hyperplane) between the instances of different classes based on the principle of maximizing the margin. Due to this principle, the generalization error of SVM is theoretically independent from the instance's dimension [Kha+16b]. For example, consider a case of a two-class classification problem where a given set of labeled training instances $(x_i, y_i), x_i \in \mathbb{R}$ and $y_i = \{-1, +1\}$ is provided. That is, the positive instances are associated with label $y_i = +1$ and the negative instances have labels $y_i = -1$. During the training, the objective function of the SVM penalize the violations of margin using a slack variable (ξ). In the classical SVM solver, the objective is to learn a parameter w to determine the hyperplane between a set of objects having different classes. However, the training process in the propose technique aims to estimate the optimal value of β which is similar to w but consists of set of part filters and their spatial relations. To learn these parameters, the following optimization problem is solved:

$$arg \min_{\beta} \frac{1}{2} \| \beta \|^2 + C(\sum_{pos} \xi_{pos} + \sum_{neg} \xi_{neg}),$$

$$s.t. \quad \beta.(I_{pos}, z) \geq 1 - \xi_{pos}, \quad \xi_{pos} \geq 0, \forall I_{pos},$$

$$\beta.(I_{neg}, z) \leq -1 + \xi_{neg}, \quad \xi_{neg} \geq 0, \forall I_{neg},$$

(5.10)

where ξ_{pos} and ξ_{neg} are representing the loss functions for positive and negative images respectively, and C is a user-defined regularization parameter which plays an important role in maximizing the margin and minimizing the loss function. To jointly learn the part-filters and their spatial relations, structSVM [Tso+04] is an optimal solution; however, the proposed method used an extension of structSVM described in [Ram13]. Similar to liblinear implementation of SVM [Fan+08b], it uses a dual coordinate descent method to find an optimal solution of the objective function in a single pass. In particular, it split the problem into a series of sub-problems and proceed by optimizing the two variables at the same time. That is, each such a sub-problem consists of two variables known as Lagrange multipliers. Coordinate descent-based optimization technique has been proven to be effective in finding the minimum of an objective function, whereas stochastic gradient descent based method may take the wrong steps along the path. Specifically, the required modification in the above derivation is the ability of linear constraints that it share the same slack variable (*i.e.*, arg $\min_{\beta,\xi_n \geq 0} \frac{1}{2} \| \beta \|^2 + C\sum_n \xi_n$ $s.t.$ $\beta.(I_n, z) \geq 1 - \xi_n, \forall_n \in pos$ and $\beta.(I_n, z) \leq -1 + \xi_n, \forall_n \in neg$) and solve the dual problem coordinate-wise. Since each negative image may have several detection windows, assigning one slack variable to each independent example may complex the learning process because each example contribute in the loss, separately. The problem would be more difficult, if the number of negative examples are exponentially large which is very common in case of structured output. In order to cope this problem, the solution proposed in [Ram13] shared the same slack variable for all the negative examples belonging to the same image I_{neg}, therefore all such negative examples may contribute only one unit to the loss function.

5.5 Experiments and Results

To the best of the author's knowledge, there is no public dataset available to analyze the movement disorders in infants. To cope with this problem, a dataset of 10 patients suffering from movement disorders is recorded in a local children hospital. The dataset was recorded using a Microsoft Kinect camera which was fitted on a tripod at the height of approximately 1.5 meter and with an angle of 90° from the table surface where the infant was lying. Figure 5.5 depicts the camera-setup during the recording. The ages of the patients are 2 weeks to 6

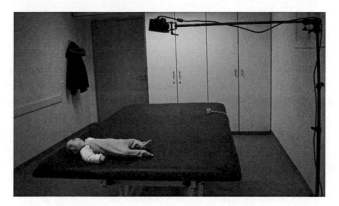

Figure 5.5: Camera setup during the recording.

months including both genders, and they were being treated in the recording days. The informed consent was obtained from all participating individuals, the infant's parents and the therapists. During the recording, the infant is lying in supine position (*i.e.*, lying on back) on the table, wearing only diapers which helps to clearly capture the movements. The recording was held when the patients are active and performing some movements. For each patient, the recording session usually lasted around 15 minutes and a total of 20 video sequences are recorded for 10 patients which comprises more than 25,000 frames.

In order to train a model, 650 positive images are selected to prepare a training set. Moreover, the training images are flipped and rotated between -15° to +15° with an interval of 5°. The rotation and flipping process helps the model to learn various possible states of the body parts hence, makes the model robust. To encode the states of a particular part, its relative location with the respective parent-part in all the training images is clustered. The cluster size S is chosen based on the degree of articulation in that part. In particular, the parts with a large degree of articulations require more part-filters for accurate detection. The cluster sizes are validated with Bayesian information criterion (BIC) to estimate the optimal value of S for each body part. The BIC criterion (also known as Schwarz criterion) uses the likelihood of the data given by the model (*i.e.*, clusters) and the complexity of the model to select an optimal one among a finite set of models. The BIC value can be computed as [Kha+18c]:

$$\text{BIC} = -2 \cdot \ln\left(\frac{R}{n}\right) + k \cdot \ln(n), \tag{5.11}$$

where the first term in Equation 5.11 describe the likelihood of data given by the model and it consists of n which is the number of instances in the training dataset and R representing the residual sum of squares [Kha+18c]. The second term describes the complexity of the model where $k = S(d + 1)$ and d is the dimension of the data. The proposed technique computes the BIC value for each model (*i.e.*, body part) with different number of clusters sizes S, and the optimal size is selected. In particular, the size of S is set to 4 for head and neck, 9 for elbows, 8 for hands and knees, and 6 for the rest of body parts. It is experimentally observed too that increasing the number of clusters does not improve the detection accuracy, however it instead adversely affects the computational time of the algorithm. The deformation parameter is initialized with $[0,0,0.01,0.01]$ which demonstrates the part location to be very close to its rest location. The negative images with no human subjects are also used in the training set. Each possible root location in the negative image demonstrates a unique negative example in the training set. The trained model is evaluated using a probe set which comprises the rest of the video sequences. The performance of the proposed algorithm is evaluated using two challenging matrices, and the movement at different predicted joints are also compared with manually annotated ground truth information. The short description of each evaluation matrix and the comparison of achieved results with existing techniques are summarized in the following.

Performance Evaluation using Average Joint Position Error

Since the accuracy of motion capturing in the proposed algorithm is based on parts detection which are located at joints, the joint estimation accuracy of the proposed algorithm is measured to demonstrate its detection performance. The average joint position error (AJPE) metric measures the average error of the difference between the predicted joint locations and their ground truth information. Table 5.1 presents the result achieved by the proposed algorithm and their comparison with existing state-of-the-art technique. The results reveal

Table 5.1: Average joint position error (in millimeter) per body part. The subscripts R and L are denoting the right and the left body part, respectively.

Method	Head	Neck	$Shoulder_R$	$Shoulder_L$	$Elbow_R$	$Elbow_L$	$Hand_R$	
[Hes+15]	37.0	20.0	27.0	73.0	24.0	20.0	44.0	
Proposed	20.3	11.4	11.0	11.4	11.2	12.4	11.9	
Method	$Hand_L$	Hip_R	Hip_L	$Knee_R$	$Knee_L$	$Foot_R$	$Foot_L$	Mean
[Hes+15]	149.0	33.0	12.0	45.0	49.0	28.0	30.0	41.0
Proposed	14.4	11.9	11.2	11.9	11.7	14.0	12.8	12.7

that the proposed algorithm outperforms the existing method in the detection of all body parts with the lowest AJPE of 12.7 millimeters.

Performance Evaluation using Wost Case Accuracy

Wost case accuracy (WCA) metric measures the percentage of frames in which all of the joints must be detected within a certain threshold distance (Ω_{wca}) from the ground truth information. It is worth mentioning that any frame/object having an error on even one joint location larger than Ω_{wca}, would be considered as false positive. Similar to [Hes+17], two evaluations are performed using Ω_{wca} as 5 Centimeters (cm) and 3 cm. Table 5.2 summarizes the results achieved by the proposed algorithm and their comparison with existing method. The results reveal that the proposed algorithm outperforms the compared method in both evaluations.

Table 5.2: Performance evaluation of the proposed method using WCA

Method	$\Omega_{wca} = 5cm$	$\Omega_{wca} = 3cm$
[Hes+17]	90.0%	85.0%
Proposed	95.8%	86.3%

Performance Evaluation using Captured Motion Information

The performance of the proposed algorithm is also evaluated using the computed motion information at different joints such as elbows, shoulders, knees, *etc.* Since the computed motion information is based on angle orientations at joints, they are compared with the ground truth angles. Figure 5.6 presents the computed motion information in comparison with the ground truth orientations. The overlapped area in Figure 5.6 demonstrates the similar movement patterns. Despite the fact that there are little variations in the computed and the ground truth movement patterns, it can be observed that the computed angle orientations precisely reflect the ground truth orientations. The proposed method estimates the joint position as the center location of predicted body part and computes edges between the estimated locations to measure the angle orientations. Therefore, the deviation of part-filter window by few pixels around the actual location of body part generates such variations in computing the angles (Figure 5.6). The plotted information can help the doctors and the therapists to get an impression of any movement disorders based on the absence of specific motion information in the body part.

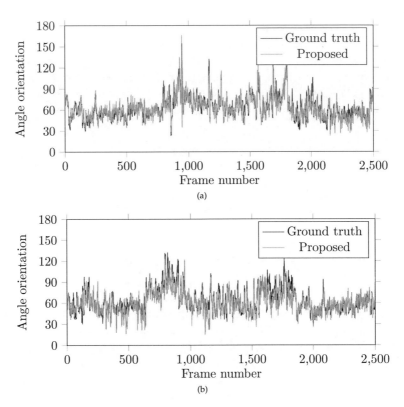

Figure 5.6: Predicted and ground truth angle orientations on a test video sequence with 2,500 frames. (a) Angle orientations at left arm, and (b) angle orientations at right arm.

5.6   Summary

This chapter introduced a vision-based framework to analyze the movement disorders in
infants. First, a model is learned using a set of training images to detect the infant's skeleton
information. The proposed model is represented using a tree-structured graph and the
learning process is described in Section 5.4. Second, the detection of different body parts
using the learned model is outlined in Section 5.2. Finally, the computation of angles at
different predicted joint locations and their tracking in the temporal direction to encode the
motion information is presented in Section 5.3. The experimental evaluation is carried out
on the collected database and the results are discussed in Section 5.5.

Chapter 6

Evaluation of the Therapeutic Procedure

The motor disabilities arise in human due to a damage in the central nervous system, brain and spinal cord, associated with the skeletal system and control the body movement. Since the signal could not be reached from brain to affected body parts due to this damage, it introduces many problems such as, loss of movements, uncoordinated movements, failed to achieve balance and postures. The neurological physiotherapy aims to make available the message path between the brain and the musculoskeletal system by assisting the patients to perform specific movement patterns. In order to achieve this goal, the neurodevelopmental treatment and the Vojta techniques are the most common approaches used by the therapists to deal with the motor disabilities in patients [Bar96]. The neurodevelopmental treatment tends to activate the inhibits abnormal movements through positioning and handling techniques of a patient such as giving a massage, initiate a specific sleeping position, exercises of lying in prone position (*i.e.*, lying flat with the chest down and back up), which help the patient to start performing normal movements [Jun+17]. The Vojta techniques are based on the principle of reflex locomotion, which is a combination of reflex creeping in prone lying position and reflex rolling in supine lying position (*i.e.*, lying flat with the chest up and back down) and side lying positions. It enables the elementary patterns of movement in patients. The Vojta method states that a patient's central nervous system can be activated by stimulating the special reflex points on his/her body region when lying in one of the aforementioned positions. In particular, a specific stimulation is given to the patient body region to perform some reflexive movement pattern which the patient is unable to perform in a normal way. The repetitive stimulation to human body region establishe the blocked connection between the brain and the spinal cord, enabling the patient to perform these movement patterns without any external stimulation. A neurological physiotherapy is widely recommended treatment for the management of impairments which are not responsive to pharmacological treatment. It is useful to deal with the structural disorders of the muscles and joints in human.

The physiotherapy treatment can be given to the patients of any age group; however, it is found to be extremely useful for the children of age less than 1 year because most of the developmental changes take place during this time. The child is assessed in the first year of his/her life to detect any motor disability. Though at birth these movements provided by the central nervous system are initialized in a very limited way, however they can be observed very clearly within the first year of his/her life. Upon diagnosing the motor disabilities, a therapy session of 5–20 minutes is usually designed for the patient which is performed several times on daily or weekly basis. The treatment may prolong for several weeks based on the patient condition. The physiotherapy technique helps the patient to achieve better posture and more precise movements. Such techniques are found to be very useful in dealing with the diseases such as cerebral palsy, hip joint dysplasia, disturbance in central coordination, chewing and breathing problem [Kha+18a].

In order to accomplish the best outcomes, the therapist suggests the parents for in-home continuation of therapy. The therapist explains the objectives and the method of therapy process to the parents so that they can proceed with the treatment at home. The treatment program and the frequency of therapy sessions are then determined in regular intervals in accordance with the patient's development. During the therapy session, a child may start crying causing the parents worrying about their child's well-being. They might assume that the treatment is hurting their child and stop it. At this age, however, crying is an appropriate way of expression for the young patients, which after a short familiarization period becomes less and less intense [Kha+16b]. Hence, a vision-based framework is needed for monitoring the movements of the patient during therapy and assess whether they are performed correctly or not. This monitoring system can facilitate the parents by providing an accurate evaluation of an in-home therapy. It is very helpful for the individuals who do not have easy access to the therapists' clinics. Moreover, frequent visits to the therapist's clinics make the treatment expensive too, therefore in-home therapy may become an effective mode of treatment.

This chapter presents a computer-helped gadget to evaluate the therapeutic procedure by analyzing the movement patterns and poses in various body parts of the patient suffering with motor disabilities. The experimental evaluations showed that the proposed system is very effective and efficient. Moreover, it consists of few standard components and can be manufactured easily in limited budget.

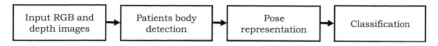

Figure 6.1: An overview of the proposed framework.

6.1 A Vision-based Framework to Evaluate the Physiotherapy

The proposed framework exploits RGBD data to analyze the accurate movements of infant body parts during the physiotherapy. It consists of three steps: First, the infant body region is automatically detected and segmented from the visual data using two novel segmentation techniques. In the first technique, the infant body region is detected from the depth image using a template matching algorithm where a human-head template is used to estimate the possible location of infant's head. The detected head location is verified using a 3D head-model fitting technique which utilizes both the edge and the relational depth change information from depth image. Upon verification, the entire body region is segmented using region growing algorithm [Kha+18a]. The second segmentation technique computes a plane equation for the table surface (where the infant is lying for therapy) and segment the infant body region from the predicted plane using k-means clustering algorithm. In both techniques, the calibration of RGB and depth frames is performed using the camera's extrinsic and intrinsic parameters to segments the infant body region from the colour image, which is used to recognize his/her lying position. The results of both segmentation techniques are quantitatively assessed. During a physiotherapy session the patient body is activated by stimulating the specific reflex points, and in a reaction one can observe some reflexive movement patterns in the upper and lower limbs of the patient (*i.e.*, Vojta's principle). In the second step of the proposed method, several features are computed from the segmented body region to analyze and represent these movements and poses. In the final step, these features are classified using a multi-class support vector machine to identify the accurate movements, which actually reveals the correctness of the given treatment. Figure 6.1 illustrates an overview of the proposed framework. The detailed description of each step is depicted in Figure 6.2 and outlined in the subsequent sections.

6.1.1 Data Pre-processing

The proposed framework exploits the depth data from Microsoft Kinect sensor to detect the infant body region. The depth sensor of the Kinect provides the depth information of the captured scene as a 2D array, known as depth image. Each pixel value in a depth image represents the distance of captured object (in millimeters) from the sensor. The proposed algorithm normalize the pixel values in the range 0–255 to achieve visualization

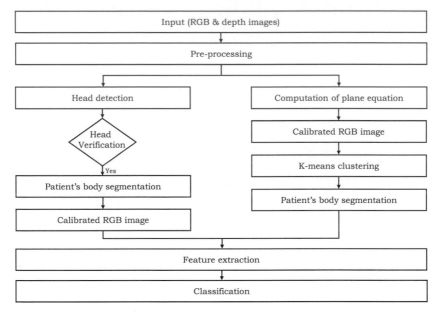

Figure 6.2: The detailed overview of the proposed framework.

and compression. Since the depth sensor of the Kinect has a limitation that it can only capture the distance information between 0.8 and 3.5 meters [Kha+16c], the corresponding pixels out of this range are filled with the offset value 0 and can be seen as random black dots in the depth image. These missing pixels are considered as noise and must be recovered to effectively used the depth information in image processing techniques [Han+13]. Considering that an image is a continuous space, the missing pixel values are recovered from the neighboring pixels using nearest neighbor interpolation algorithm.

6.1.2 Patient Body Detection

The proposed framework presents two techniques to detect and segment the patient body region from the pre-processed depth images. The detail of each technique is explained in the following.

Detection using Template Matching

This technique employs human head template to detect the patient's head region from the edge information of depth image. The edge information is computed from the depth image using Canny edge detector [Can86]. The smaller edges having length less than a predefined threshold (Ω_{edge}) are irrelevant hence, they are dropped from future processing to save the computational time. The location of the patient's head is estimated by traversing the proposed head template over the entire image in a row major order, and the best match is found. This exhaustive search is carried out only in the first frame of the video. The predicted location of the patient's body region in the current frame is used to limit the search-space in the consecutive frame.

The similarity score of the template matching is computed on each edge pixel of the depth image using the Sum of Square Differences (SSD) and Cross Correlation (CC) based algorithms [KG17]. Assuming that $\mathcal{E}$ is representing the edge image extracted from depth data and $\mathcal{T}$ is the proposed head template image with size $m \times n$ which is being matched with a rectangular region in the edge image. The SSD value S at pixel location $\mathcal{E}(x,y)$ is computed as,

$$S(x,y) = \sum_{i=1}^{m} \sum_{j=1}^{n} \left(\mathcal{E}(x+i, y+j) - \mathcal{T}(i,j) \right)^2,$$ (6.1)

where i and j represent the x and y positions of the pixel in template image $\mathcal{T}$ respectively. It can be observed from Equation 6.1 that S is a squared Euclidean distance between the image patch of $\mathcal{E}$ and the template $\mathcal{T}$ [Kha+18a]. Expanding 6.1 yields,

$$S(x,y) = \sum_{i=1}^{m} \sum_{j=1}^{n} \mathcal{E}^2(x+i, y+j) + \sum_{i=1}^{m} \sum_{j=1}^{n} \mathcal{T}^2(i,j) - 2 \sum_{i=1}^{m} \sum_{j=1}^{n} \mathcal{E}(x+i, y+j) \mathcal{T}(i,j)$$ (6.2)

Equation 6.2 consists of three terms. The first term is the sum of squared values for the patch in edge image, the second term is associated with the template image, and the third term is twice the correlation between the patch of edge image $\mathcal{E}$ and the template $\mathcal{T}$. It can be noticed from Equation 6.2 that the Euclidean distance between the patch of $\mathcal{E}$ and $\mathcal{T}$ would be decreased when their similarity (*i.e.*, correlation) is increased. This also gives an intuition to use correlation as similarity measure. Additionally, the second term in Equation 6.2 (*i.e.*, $\sum_{i=1}^{m} \sum_{j=1}^{n} \mathcal{T}^2(i,j)$) is constant and the first term (*i.e.*, $\sum_{i=1}^{m} \sum_{j=1}^{n} \mathcal{E}^2(x+i, y+j)$) is approximately constant [GGB84; Del+17]. The rest of the third term is the cross correlation. That is,

$$CC(x,y) = \sum_{i=1}^{m} \sum_{j=1}^{n} \mathcal{E}(x+i, y+j) \mathcal{T}(i,j), \quad (6.3)$$

where CC represents the cross correlation which can be computed by taking the inner product of image patch and template. The computation of cross correlation in spatial domain is much expensive [Lyo10]. For example, in a given image of size $M \times M$ and a template of size $N \times N$, the computation of cross correlation requires $N^2(M-N+1)^2$ additions and $N^2(M-N+1)^2$ multiplications [Lew95]. In order to avoid this computational overhead, the proposed detection technique computes the cross correlation in frequency domain using fast Fourier transform (FFT) [BB88] and correlation theorem [Nus12] which states that multiplying the Fourier transform of one function (*i.e.*, $\mathcal{T}$) by the complex conjugate of the Fourier transform of the second function (*i.e.*, $\mathcal{E}$) provides the Fourier transform of their correlation. That is,

$$CC(u,v) = \mathcal{F}^{-1}\Big(\mathcal{F}^*(\mathcal{E}(x,y)) . \mathcal{F}(\mathcal{T}(i,j))\Big), \quad (6.4)$$

where $\mathcal{F}^{-1}$ represents the inverse Fourier transform, $\mathcal{F}^*(\mathcal{E}(x,y))$ is the complex conjugate of the Fourier transform of edge image $\mathcal{E}$ and $\mathcal{F}(\mathcal{T}(i,j))$ is the Fourier transform of template image $\mathcal{T}$. With the aforementioned sizes of a given image and template, the computational cost of CC in frequency domain is $18M^2 \log_2 M$ real additions and $12M^2 \log_2 M$ real multiplications [Lew95]. Its is empirically concluded that the computation of correlation either in spatial domain or in frequency domain does not influence the performance of the proposed detection technique; however, the computation in frequency domain is 2.5 to 12 times faster than in spatial domain [Kha+18a].

The size of the head may vary from child to child and it is also based on the distance from the camera because a child's head close to camera would be characterized by a large region in the image compared to the one at a far distance. Although the angle orientation of camera and its distance from the table surface is pre-defined (outlined in Section 6.1.5), however the detection is performed in a multi-resolution fashion which makes the detection algorithm robust to change in scale. The template matching results introduced few high-scoring locations in $\mathcal{E}$ as possible head regions. However, all the detected regions may not necessarily contain the head. To cope with this issue, the detected regions are verified for human head through a 3D model fitting technique. The proposed detection technique constructs a 3D hemisphere model [XCA11; KG17] for the head verification. The highest scoring head location that also verified by the 3D hemisphere model, is selected as a correct estimation. To extract the patient body region, the region growing algorithm is applied on the verified head location. The region growing algorithm seeks the seed point (*i.e.*, head

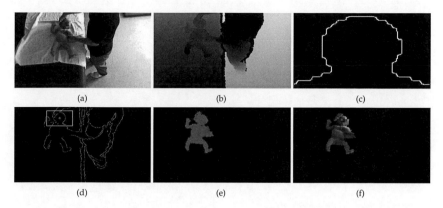

Figure 6.3: Results of proposed detection technique on a sample depth image using template matching. (a) a manipulated colour image (*i.e.*, converted to grayscale); (b) corresponding depth image of (a); (c) the template used for head detection; (d) head location after verification; (e) segmented body region in depth image; (f) corresponding body region in RGB image (converted to grayscale) which is obtained after calibration.

location) and grow the region around it by measuring the similarity of neighboring pixels. All those pixels having the similarity more than a pre-defined threshold $\Omega_{similar}$ are selected as patient's body region. The propose detection technique employs camera's extrinsic and intrinsic parameters to segment the corresponding patient's body region from the colour image.

The results of the proposed detection technique is depicted in Figure 6.3. A sample colour and its corresponding depth image are shown in Figure 6.3a and Figure 6.3b, respectively. The proposed human head template is presented in Figure 6.3c. The dot in the rectangle in Figure 6.3d shows the best matching location which is verified using a 3D hemisphere model. The extracted patient's body region from the depth image and its corresponding colour image is shown in Figure 6.3e and Figure 6.3f, respectively. As described earlier that an exhaustive search is performed only for the first frame of the video; in the succeeding frames instead of traversing the head template again on the entire image the proposed detection technique exploits the temporal information of the detected patient location. Similar to data recording for the movement analysis of infants (Chapter 5), the camera was fixed during the therapy process and patients are not making any rapid movements. Therefore, the predicted location of patient in the current frame with the relaxation of a certain threshold pixels (Ω_{dist}) in all directions, is used to set the search-space in the succeeding frame.

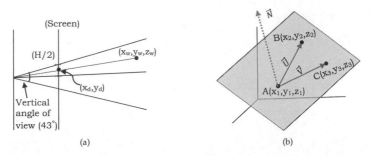

(a)   (b)

Figure 6.4: (a) An example of illustrating the projection of a depth image pixel in a real world coordinate system. (b) Computing the vectors required for the plane equation.

Detection using Plane Equation

In the second detection technique, the plane equation of the table surface in depth image is computed where an infant is lying for therapy. The detected table surface is used to segment the infant's body region in the later step. Since the camera and table are fixed during the recording (Section 6.1.5), the table surface remains in the same plane during the recording. The proposed technique requires three points on the table surface which must neither be on a child's body region nor on a single line (*i.e.*, collinear). The marking of these points is required only for once in the first frame of the video as the recording setup remains fixed afterwards. The corresponding world coordinates of three selected pixel locations are computed using their depth values. Assuming that d and w represent the subscripts for depth and world respectively. That is, a point in depth image can be represented as (x_d, y_d) and the corresponding point in the real world would be (x_w, y_w, z_w) (Figure 6.4a). Using a given depth value z at a selected location, the x and y real world coordinates for a given pixel location (i, j) are determined using the following equations [Kha+18a]:

$$x_w = 2tan(\frac{\theta_h}{2})(j - \frac{\mathcal{H}}{2})\frac{z}{\mathcal{H}} \tag{6.5}$$

$$y_w = 2tan(\frac{\theta_v}{2})(i - \frac{\mathcal{V}}{2})\frac{z}{\mathcal{V}} \tag{6.6}$$

where $\mathcal{H}$ and $\mathcal{V}$ represent the number of horizontal and vertical pixels in the field of view, respectively. Additionally, θ_h and θ_v are representing the horizontal and vertical viewing angles of the Kinect camera (Figure 6.4a), which are 57° and 43°(Kinect V$_1$), respectively. These corresponding real world points are used to compute the plane equation of table surface. Assuming that these points are denoted as $A(x_1, y_1, z_1)$, $B(x_2, y_2, z_2)$ and $C(x_3, y_3, z_3)$.

The proposed technique forms two vectors $\vec{U}$ (from A to B) and $\vec{V}$ (from A to C) using the following equations (Figure 6.4b):

$$\vec{U} = \overrightarrow{AB} = B - A \tag{6.7}$$

$$\vec{V} = \overrightarrow{AC} = C - A \tag{6.8}$$

It can be observed from the Figure 6.4b that $\vec{U}$ and $\vec{V}$ are both located on the same plane and also parallel to the plane; therefore, a normal vector $\vec{N}$ which would be perpendicular to the plane, can be computed by taking the cross product of $\vec{U}$ and $\vec{V}$. That is,

$$\vec{N} = \vec{U} \times \vec{V} = (B - A) \times (C - A) \tag{6.9}$$

Since $\vec{N}$ is orthogonal to the plane, it would be orthogonal to any vector too that lies in the same plane. The dot product of the normal vector and a vector on the plane becomes the equation of the plane [Pla]. Additionally, the dot product of two orthogonal vectors is zero (i.e., $\vec{N} \cdot \vec{U} = 0$). Therefore, using any of the three given points, the equation of the plane can be written as,

$$\langle a, b, c \rangle \cdot (\langle x - x_o, y - y_o, z - z_o \rangle) = 0 \tag{6.10}$$

Expanding Equation 6.10 yields:

$$a(x - x_n) + b(y - y_n) + c(z - z_n) = 0, \tag{6.11}$$

where a, b and c are the components of the normal vector $\vec{N}$ and (x_o, y_o, z_o) is a given point on the plane which can be any of the point in $\{A, B, C\}$. Equation 6.11 is known as the scalar equation of the plane (or the Cartesian form of the plane equation) and can be written as,

$$ax + by + cz = d \tag{6.12}$$

where $d = ax_o + by_o + cz_o$. Equation 6.12 is considered as the equation of plane which can be used to identify the table surface pixels in the depth image. In order to segment the table surface, all the pixels in depth image are evaluated using the above mentioned equation. In particular, the pixel values which satisfy the plane equation within a certain threshold range are extracted and the remaining are discarded. This process may introduce few holes in the extracted table surface due to depth inaccuracy of the sensor [Cho+14]. To cope with

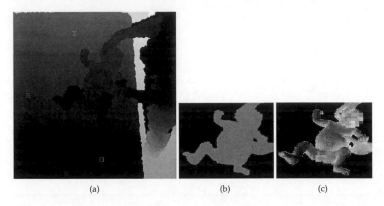

(a)   (b)   (c)

Figure 6.5: (a) Marking of sample points on the table surface to compute a plane equation; (b) segmented body region in depth image; (c) segmented body region in the corresponding RGB image (a manipulated colour image *i.e.*, converted to grayscale).

this problem, the proposed technique exploits a hole filling algorithm [Soi13] to estimate the missing pixels values. In case more than one regions are extracted, it uses connected component algorithm to select the largest region which demonstrates the table surface. At this stage, the corresponding region from RGB image is also segmented using the camera's extrinsic and intrinsic parameters and K-means clustering algorithm is employed on it with skin colour as observation to segment the patient's body region. The results of the proposed technique are presented in Figure 6.5. The marking of three sample points on a depth image for the computation of plane equation is illustrated in Figure 6.5a. The segmented patient's body region from the depth and the corresponding RGB images are shown in Figure 6.5b and Figure 6.5c, respectively.

6.1.3   Pose Representation

As mentioned earlier that the physiotherapy is given to the patients in prone, supine, and side lying positions. In the proposed study, the data is recorded when the patient is lying for the treatment in prone and supine positions. During the therapy process a specific stimulation is given to the patient's body region to perform some reflexive movement pattern. In particular, after repetitive stimulation one can observe these movements in the upper and lower limbs of the patient. These movements are carefully analyzed and a set of nine features is designed to represent these movements in the aforementioned lying positions. The movements of

Table 6.1: Limbs movement classes. Label is class label.

Label	Movements
ω_1	Upper limbs movement in prone lying position.
ω_2	Lower limbs movement in prone lying position.
ω_3	Upper limbs movement in supine lying position.
ω_4	Lower limbs movement in supine lying position.

upper and lower limbs in both lying positions are distributed into four groups and their description is outlined in Table 6.1.

Since a depth image does not acquire the detailed structure of the scene, it is very difficult to recognize the lying position of a child from the segmented region of depth image (Figure 6.5b and Figure 6.3e). The proposed algorithm employ the corresponding segmented region from RGB image to detect the lying position of the patient, using the face detection algorithm [VJ01] on it. In order to capture the described movements (Table 6.1), the bounding box of the whole segmented region from the depth image is divided into two equally-high sub-boxes, as depicted in Figure 6.6. Assuming that u and l are denoting the subscripts for the bounding-box in the upper region and the lower region respectively, h represents the height and w is the width, the description of the computed features is outlined in Table 6.2. The 9-dimensional feature vector F is constructed as,

$$F = [F_1, F_2, F_3, F_4, F_5, F_6, F_7, F_8, F_9] \tag{6.13}$$

6.1.4 Classification

The computed features are classified using a SVM. The proposed method uses *LIBSVM* library [CL11] to implement SVM with RBF kernel (also known as Gaussian kernel). In particular, it exploits the formulation of C-support vector with the soft margin parameter C (as described in Section 3.1.5) and γ when RBF kernels is used as meta-parameter. The parameter γ of RBF kernel specifies the spreadness of the kernel. The *LIBSVM* employs one-against-one approach to solve the multi-class classification problem [CL11]. Specifically, in a given set of classes it uses two-class SVM for each pair. For example, for a given set of N classes it constructs $N(N-1)/2$ two-class classifiers. It employs voting strategy to choose the class label for a given test instance. Hence, the test instance is classified to the class with the maximum number of votes. The proposed method performed 5-fold cross validation

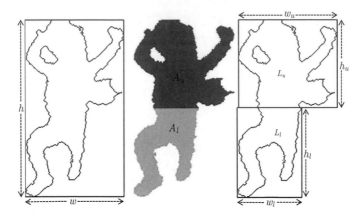

Figure 6.6: An example of illustrating the feature computation. Shape bounding box and equally-high sub-boxes (*i.e.*, $h_u = h_l$) are used for feature extraction. The description of the feature computation is described in Table 6.2.

Table 6.2: Description of nine features to represent the pose. F denotes the feature and V describes the computation of features.

F	V	Feature Description
F_1		The lying position of a child.
F_2	$\frac{h_u}{w_u}$	The ratio of height and width in upper bounding box.
F_3	$\frac{h_l}{w_l}$	The ratio of height and width in lower bounding box.
F_4	$\frac{h}{w}$	The ratio of height and width in complete bounding box.
F_5	A_u	The area in upper bounding box.
F_6	A_l	The area in lower bounding box.
F_7	L_u	The length of the contour in upper bounding box.
F_8	L_l	The length of the contour in lower bounding box.
F_9	$A_u + A_l$	The sum of area in upper and lower bounding box.

to validate the model with the selection of soft margin parameter C and γ, prior to train the actual model on the full training dataset. That is, the training instances are randomly distributed into five subsets and training was performed five times; each time leaving one partition out of the training process which is used for testing.

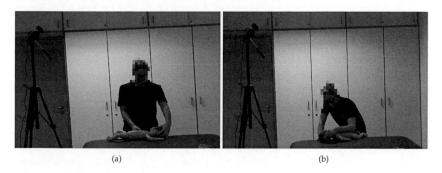

(a)   (b)

Figure 6.7: Recording setup and an illustration of the therapy process. (a) Supine position, and (b) prone position.

6.1.5   Experiments and Results

Dataset acquisition

To the best of the author's knowledge, there is no public dataset available to analyze the movements of patients during the physiotherapy. Therefore, a dataset of 10 patients is collected in a local children hospital. The ages of the patients are between 2 weeks and 6 months including both genders. The informed consent was obtained from all participating individuals, the infant's parents and the therapists.

The dataset is recorded using a Microsoft Kinect camera which was fitted on a tripod at height of approximately 2 meters and with an angle of 45° from the table surface where the patient is lying for therapy. The reason to choose this camera setting is to capture the best data quality with minimum occlusion, particularly when therapy is given in prone position. Figure 6.7 depicts the therapy process in both prone and supine positions, and the camera-setup during the recording. A therapy session usually lasted between 15–20 minutes for each patient, and both of the colour and the depth frames were recorded. Upon careful analysis, more than 15,000 frames are selected which comprises the useful information of upper and lower limbs movement during the treatment. Figure 6.8 demonstrate the various limbs movements of a patient during the physiotherapy.

Performance Analysis

The performance of the proposed method is evaluated for both of the patient detection and the accuracy of classification using the proposed features. The outcomes are discussed in the following sections.

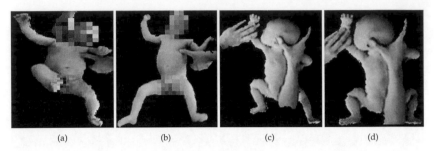

Figure 6.8: Sample images (manipulated colour images to grayscale) depicting the various movement patterns in patient body during therapy. (a)-(b):limbs movement in supine lying position; (c)-(d): limbs movement in prone lying position.

Detection Accuracy

Both detection algorithms are evaluated on the recorded dataset quantitatively and their results are compared. There are four possible outcomes of a detection algorithm, namely true positives (TP), false positive (FP), true negative (TN) and false negative (FN). True positive indicate to the number of predicted positive instances that were correct and the FP is the number of predicted positive instances that were incorrect. Similarly, TN and FN indicate to the number of predicted negative instances that were correct and incorrect, respectively [Kha+18a]. The performance of the proposed detection techniques is evaluated using five different metrics: Sensitivity, Specificity, Positive Predictive Value (PPV) or Precision, Negative Predictive Value (NPV), and Accuracy [Far+17]. The Confidence Intervals (CI) of each measure is also computed to estimate the range of values which is likely to contain the population parameter of interest. Confidence intervals are computed at confidence level of 95%. The results are outlined in Table 6.3 and computed as follows:

$$\text{Sensitivity} = \frac{TP}{TP + FN}$$
$$\text{Specificity} = \frac{TN}{TN + FP}$$
$$\text{PPV or Precision} = \frac{TP}{TP + FP}$$
$$\text{NPV} = \frac{TN}{TN + FN}$$
$$\text{Accuracy or Detection Rate} = \frac{TP + TN}{TP + FN + TN + FP}$$

The results reveal that the detection technique using plane equation perform better than

Table 6.3: Performance analysis of the proposed detection techniques in terms of Sensitivity, Specificity, PPV, NPV and Accuracy. The values in parenthesis represent the 95% confidence interval CI for each measure.

Measure	Template matching technique	Plane equation technique
Sensitivity	86.01 (85.2, 86.8)	98.20 (97.9, 98.5)
Specificity	80.93 (80.0, 81.8)	95.71 (95.2, 96.2)
PPV	79.68 (78.9, 80.4)	96.10 (95.7, 96.5)
NPV	86.93 (86.3, 87.6)	98.02 (97.7, 98.3)
Accuracy	83.29 (82.7, 83.9)	97.00 (96.7, 97.3)

template matching based technique. It perform better in terms of all performance metrics. The reason for the drop in accuracy of head template matching technique is due to the occlusion at the patient's head region. This situation is observed in few cases when the patient is lying in supine position and sometimes in prone position too, and the head region is either partially visible or totally occluded by the therapist.

Classification Accuracy

The dataset is distributed into four classes (outlined in Table 6.1) to assess the classification performance of the proposed features. The features are computed from each segmented body-region (Section 6.1.3) and their values are normalized in the range $[-1, +1]$. The reason to use normalization is to avoid elements in greater numeric ranges dominating those in smaller numeric ranges. This process is also useful to avoid the numerical difficulties during

Table 6.4: Summary of classification results. The recognition results for the corresponding class are highlighted in boldface.

Reference	Predicted			
	ω_1	ω_2	ω_3	ω_4
ω_1	**80.16**	19.50	0.17	0.17
ω_2	55.00	**44.84**	0.16	0
ω_3	0	0	**91.33**	8.67
ω_4	0	0	4.00	**96.00**

Average Accuracy: **78.08**

the calculation *e.g.* kernel values usually depend on the inner product of feature vectors, and large attribute values may cause numerical problems [Kha+18a]. The classification results are summarized in Table 6.4 which demonstrate the performance of the proposed features to discriminatively define the movement patterns or poses of a patient during therapy in aforementioned positions (Table 6.1). The classification results show that the proposed features can effectively encode all the respective poses except in ω_2 where the performance is degraded drastically. The reason for this drop in the accuracy is that a significant portion of the patient's lower limbs is occluded by the therapist's arm, as depicted in Figure 6.8c– 6.8d. Though the proposed algorithm is able to detect the patient's lying position, however the estimation of lower limbs become ambiguous. The proposed algorithm achieved an average classification accuracy of 78% in this initial study.

6.2   A Deformable Part-based Model to Evaluate the Physiotherapy

An interesting application to assess the accuracy of the patient's movement patterns during physiotherapy is built based upon the technique proposed in Chapter 5. The human body structure is detected from an image using the part-filters and the spatial relations between the parts. To encode the part movements, the angles between connected parts are computed at predicted joint locations and their orientation is tracked temporally. The temporal variation in the orientation of a joint is used to estimate the recovery progress of a patient.

Although the deformable part-based model has demonstrated excellent results in estimating the movements of infants (Section 5.5), however during physiotherapy few body parts of the patient are always occluded by the therapist (Figure 6.8 – 6.9). In particular, it can be observe that half of the patient's body region is consistently occluded by the therapist's arm when therapy is given in prone position. Since the part-based model detection technique uses a tree-structured graph to evaluate the spatial relations between the parts, a confusion may arise if any intermediate parts in the structure are not detectable due to occlusion resulting in increase in false alarms. To overcome this problem, the desired movement patterns are localized in both of the supine and prone positions using two different models, which are learned separately for each of the lying positions and the computation of angle orientation is performed on desired joint locations rather than on the complete body. In particular, a full-body model is learned for supine position similar to the technique described in Section 5.1. However, for prone position the movements of the lower limbs are captured. The model for prone position encodes the body structure from ankle joint (*i.e.*, leaf node) to hip joint (*i.e.*, root node), and the motion information at the knee joint is computed.

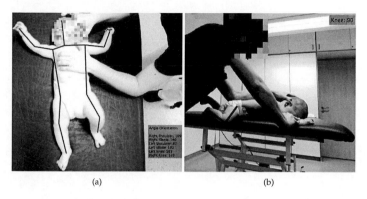

(a)   (b)

Figure 6.9: An example illustrating the movement capturing at predicted joint locations during therapy. (a) Angle orientations at different joints in supine position, (b) angle orientation at the knee joint in prone position.

Figure 6.9 depicts the estimation of poses and movements in both lying positions. For prone position, the angle orientation is computed only at the knee joint.

6.3 Summary

This chapter introduced a vision-based framework to evaluate the therapeutic procedure using two different methods. The first method is presented in Section 6.1 which is based on detecting the human body region in RGBD data using template matching and plane equation techniques. Different features are computed from the segmented body region to estimate the accurate poses of the patient during the therapy process and they are classified into their respective classes using SVM. The second method is presented in Section 6.2 which exploits the deformable part-based model technique to detect different body parts and estimate the patient poses during the treatment.

Chapter 7

Conclusion and Future Work

This chapter presents a comprehensive summary of the introduced gait recognition techniques and the algorithms based on movement analysis. The conclusion is drawn based on the facts which are obtained during the implementation and evaluation of the presented work. Lastly, an insight into possible future work is discussed to improve the proposed techniques and draw new directions.

7.1 Conclusion

Recently, biometrics has become a popular research area due to its widespread acceptance in many computer vision based applications to provide the legitimate authentication of identity for an individual such as surveillance, forensic, and access control. The first part of this dissertation addressed the problem of person identification from visual data using their walking styles. Gait is an emerging biometric modality which can be used to recognize an individual based on his/her walking style. Acquisition in a non-invasive and hidden manner without any interaction with the system distinguishes gait from the other biometrics. However, gait recognition is challenging as it depends on various physiological, psychological and external factors: clothing, walking speed, walking surface, footwear, carrying objects, viewing angle, mood and illness.

Three novel gait recognition techniques are proposed in this dissertation. The first method is presented in Section 3.1 which uses the spatial and the temporal characteristics of walk for individual recognition. This method is superior than most existing gait recognition algorithms because its performance is independent of human silhouette segmentation and gait-cycle estimation. The local motion features are computed directly from the video sequence of walk and encoded into a high level representation using a codebook based approach, and their discriminative ability is measured using a simple linear SVM. The second gait recognition method is presented in Section 3.2 flourishes the idea of using a generic codebook for gait recognition. Instead of constructing a separate codebook for each dataset, the idea is to construct a single, shared and generic codebook from one dataset which can be used to encode the features of other relevant datasets. To this end, an extensive evaluation is carried out to find a dataset encompassing the diversity of walking styles. The proposed generic codebook is used to encode the gait sequences of different datasets and it achieved very convincing performance (Section 3.2). Gait recognition under varying viewpoint is challenging because the appearance of an individual's walk changes heavily due to the change in viewing angle. Furthermore, it is unavoidable in real-world surveillance systems too. In Chapter 4, a cross-view gait recognition technique is presented which is build using the spatiotemporal gait representation proposed in Chapter 3. The technique is based on VTM and constructs a deep neural network which learns a model to map the gait sequences of different viewpoints to the same canonical view. The learning process is performed using a pretty small, unlabeled set of training instances. Moreover, the proposed technique learns a single model to transform the gait sequences from all different viewpoints to the same canonical view rather than learning a separate model for each view-pair. The cross-view gait representation of testing instances are obtained using the learned model which are classified using a simple linear SVM. All the three proposed gait recognition techniques are tested on standard gait datasets. The evaluations showed very convincing results, outperforming large number of competing methods.

The second part of this dissertation presents the research related to the movement analysis of human body parts. The movements of human body parts generate numerous number of activity patterns which can be detected and analyzed. In particular, its applications in clinical assessment and evaluation systems are presented in this dissertation. A framework to analyze the movement disorders in infants is presented in Chapter 5. It detects different body parts based on joint locations and computes angles at the predicted joints. The orientation information at joints in the temporal direction is used to encode the respective motion information. The human body structure is detected by employing a set of part-filters and the spatial relation between the parts, represented using a tree-structured graph. The learning is performed using a structured support vector machine. The experimental evaluation carried out on a dataset collected in a local children hospital showed promising results. A computer vision based system to evaluate the therapeutic procedure using RGBD data is presented in Chapter 6. Two methods are proposed to monitor the accurate movements of the subject in physiotherapy. The method outlined in Section 6.1, extracts the subject's body region using two novel techniques. The first is template matching based and the second relies on a background segmentation method using plane equation. Several features are computed from the segmented body region to represent the poses and movement patterns in human body during the physiotherapy, which are classified using SVM. The second method described in Section 6.2 is based on deformable part-based model (Chapter 5) to detect different body parts and estimate the patient's pose by computing angle orientation at desired joint locations. The experimental evaluation of these methods performed on a challenging dataset demonstrate their effectiveness.

7.2   Future Work

The research presented in this dissertation opened new horizons, unexplored areas, and exciting directions of investigation.

- One interesting investigation would be the fusion of gait with other biometric modalities such as face for improved authentication. The integration of these features may provide better non-intrusive verification, with interesting applications *e.g.* a smart-gate based application for access control which usually uses iris and face biometrics for authentication. The main limitation of such a systems is that they require individuals to be captured in near-field. However, replacing iris with the gait (*i.e.*, face and gait based system) can provide a robust and distance-field capturing system that can work more effectively in a hidden manner. Nonetheless, combining gait with face biometrics require to place the camera where frontal view can be captured. An inquisition of fusion strategies can be useful to achieve the best performance.

- The proposed gait characteristics can be explored to assess the onset of the frailty syndrome and fall detection in elderly people. The analysis of gait to identify important features and assessment protocols can pave the way to build an automatic tool for the early prevention of fall and the risk of frailty. In particular, an unusual variation in the gait patterns of a walker can be further analyzed to estimate the fall. Besides the gait speed of a person, the analysis of increase in the gait variability over the time period can be exploited for frailty assessment.

- The VTM based approaches have proven to be effective in learning the mapping of data obtained from one viewpoint to a relatively close target viewpoint. However, they perform rather poor when the distance between the two viewpoints is large. Hence, one possible solution would be to explore a two-step transformations for such viewpoints. In this way, all the training viewpoints are grouped into two or more parts and each of the VTM would learn a mapping of gait sequences from different viewpoints belonging to one particular part.

- It is observed during the therapy process that most of the patient body region is occluded by the therapist's arm, which may cause confusion during the detection and classification of movements. To this end, a multi-camera setup would be an interesting investigation which also facilitates to monitor the movements in 3D domain. Moreover, a more sophisticated model (*e.g.* CNN) should be employed to increase the detection accuracy of body parts. For this purpose, a large dataset of the patients during the therapy should be captured. The proposed technique should be extended for adult patients with the inclusion of few wireless motion sensors such as IMUs to capture the respective movements. The information of motion sensors can be used to validate the performance of the proposed markerless technique.

Abbreviations

1D	one dimensional 17
2D	two dimensional 6, 9, 17–21, 39, 90
3D	three dimensional 6, 7, 15, 19–21, 28, 29, 89, 93
CC	Cross Correlation 91
CCTV	closed-circuit television 2, 6, 19
CI	Confidence Intervals 100, 101
CNN	Convolutional Neural Network 18, 22, 111
f/s	frames-per-second 23, 24, 69
FK	Fisher kernel 40
FV	Fisher vector 36–38, 40, 41, 55
GEI	gait energy image 16, 22, 33, 57, 58
GMA	General Movement Assessment 4, 73
GMM	Gaussian mixture model 36, 37, 41, 53, 55
HOF	Histogram of Optical Flow 17, 34, 35
HOG	Histogram of Oriented Gradient 17, 34–36, 38, 75, 76, 80
IMU	Inertial Measurement Units 7, 26, 30, 31, 111
leakyReLU	Leaky Rectified Linear Unit 61, 65
MBH	Motion Boundary Histogram 34–36, 38
mocap	CMU Motion Capture 51, 52
NDNN	Non-linear Deep Neural Network 60–68, 70, 71
NPV	Negative Predictive Value 100, 101
PCA	Principal Component Analysis 39, 53, 54
PD	Parkinson's disease 31

Notation Summary

List of Figures

List of Tables

Bibliography

[Aba+16]   Martín Abadi et al. "TensorFlow: A System for Large-Scale Machine Learning." In: *OSDI*. Vol. 16. 2016, pp. 265–283.

[AC99]   Jake K Aggarwal and Quin Cai. "Human motion analysis: A review". In: *Comput. Vis. Image Underst.* 73.3 (1999), pp. 428–440.

[Aco12]   Isaac Pastor Acosta. "Upper limb rehabilitation of stroke patients using kinect and computer games". PhD thesis. School of Computing, University of Utah, 2012.

[AN12]   G. Ariyanto and M. S Nixon. "Marionette mass-spring model for 3D gait biometrics". In: *IEEE Int. Conf. Biometrics*. IEEE. 2012, pp. 354–359.

[AR11]   Jake K Aggarwal and Michael S Ryoo. "Human activity analysis: A review". In: *ACM Computing Surveys (CSUR)* 43.3 (2011), p. 16.

[Bar13]   David Barrett. *One surveillance camera for every 11 people in britain, says cctv survey*. https://www.telegraph.co.uk/technology/10172298/One-surveillance-camera-for-every-11-people-in-Britain-says-CCTV-survey.html/. [Online; accessed 01-March-2018]. 2013.

[Bar96]   Margaret J Barry. "Physical therapy interventions for patients with movement disorders due to cerebral palsy". In: *J. Child Neurol.* 11.1_suppl (1996), S51–S60.

[Bas+09]   Khalid Bashir, Tao Xiang, Shaogang Gong, and Q Mary. "Gait Representation Using Flow Fields." In: *BMVC*. 2009, pp. 1–11.

[BB88]   E Oran Brigham and E Oran Brigham. *The fast Fourier transform and its applications*. Vol. 1. prentice Hall Englewood Cliffs, NJ, 1988.

[BCD02]   Chiraz BenAbdelkader, Ross Cutler, and Larry Davis. "Person identification using automatic height and stride estimation". In: *Proc. IEEE Comput. Soc. Conf. Comput. Vis. Pattern Recognit. (CVPR)*. Vol. 4. IEEE. 2002, pp. 377–380.

[BCD04]   Chiraz BenAbdelkader, Ross G Cutler, and Larry S Davis. "Gait recognition using image self-similarity". In: *EURASIP J. Adv. Signal Process.* 2004.4 (2004), pp. 1–14.

[Ben12]   Yoshua Bengio. "Practical recommendations for gradient-based training of deep architectures". In: *Neural networks: Tricks of the trade*. Springer, 2012, pp. 437–478.

[BHP11]   Antonio Padilha Lanari Bo, Mitsuhiro Hayashibe, and Philippe Poignet. "Joint angle estimation in rehabilitation with inertial sensors and its integration with Kinect". In: *Int. Conf. Eng. Med. Biol. Soc. (EMBC)*. IEEE. 2011, pp. 3479–3483.

[BJ01]   Aaron F Bobick and Amos Y Johnson. "Gait recognition using static, activity-specific parameters". In: *Proc. IEEE Comput. Soc. Conf. Comput. Vis. Pattern Recognit. (CVPR)*. Vol. 1. IEEE. 2001, pp. I–I.

[BL05]   Jeffrey E Boyd and James J Little. "Biometric gait recognition". In: *Advanced Studies in Biometrics*. Springer, 2005, pp. 19–42.

[Ble+13]   Gabriele Bleser et al. "A personalized exercise trainer for the elderly". In: *J. Ambient Intelligence Smart Environ.* 5.6 (2013), pp. 547–562.

[BN07]   Imed Bouchrika and Mark S Nixon. "Model-based feature extraction for gait analysis and recognition". In: *Proc. IEEE Int. Conf. Comput. Vis. (ICCV)*. Springer. 2007, pp. 150–160.

[Bod+09]   Robert Bodor, Andrew Drenner, Duc Fehr, Osama Masoud, and Nikolaos Papanikolopoulos. "View-independent human motion classification using image-based reconstruction". In: *Int. J. Comput. Vis.* 27.8 (2009), pp. 1194–1206.

[Bou+11]   Imed Bouchrika, Michaela Goffredo, John Carter, and Mark Nixon. "On using gait in forensic biometrics". In: *J. Forensic Sci.* 56.4 (2011), pp. 882–889.

[Bry+06]   C Bryanton, J Bosse, Marie Brien, Jennifer Mclean, Anna McCormick, and Heidi Sveistrup. "Feasibility, motivation, and selective motor control: virtual reality compared to conventional home exercise in children with cerebral palsy". In: *Cyberpsychology Behav.* 9.2 (2006), pp. 123–128.

[Bur+08]   JW Burke, PJ Morrow, MDJ McNeill, SM McDonough, and DK Charles. "Vision based games for upper-limb stroke rehabilitation". In: *Int. Conf. Mach. Vis. Image Process. (IMVIP)*. IEEE. 2008, pp. 159–164.

[BXG08]   Khalid Bashir, Tao Xiang, and Shaogang Gong. "Feature Selection for Gait Recognition without Subject Cooperation". In: *BMVC*. 2008, pp. 1–10.

[BXG09]   Khalid Bashir, Tao Xiang, and Shaogang Gong. "Gait recognition using gait entropy image". In: *IET ICDP*. 2009, pp. 1–6.

[BXG10a]   K. Bashir, T. Xiang, and S. Gong. "Bashir, Khalid and Xiang, Tao and Gong, Shaogang". In: *BMVC*. 2010, pp. 1–11.

[BXG10b]   Khalid Bashir, Tao Xiang, and Shaogang Gong. "Gait recognition without subject cooperation". In: *Pattern Recognit. Lett.* 31.13 (2010), pp. 2052–2060.

[Can86]   John Canny. "A Computational Approach to Edge Detection". In: *IEEE Trans. Pattern Anal. Mach. Intell.* 8.6 (1986), pp. 679–698. ISSN: 0162-8828.

[Cas+16]   Francisco Manuel Castro et al. "Automatic learning of gait signatures for people identification". In: *arXiv preprint arXiv:1603.01006* (2016).

[Cas+17]   Francisco M Castro, Manuel J Marín-Jiménez, N Guil Mata, and Rafael Muñoz-Salinas. "Fisher Motion Descriptor for Multiview Gait Recognition". In: *Int. J. Pattern Recognit. Artif. Intell.* 31.01 (2017), p. 1756002.

[CCH11]   Yao-Jen Chang, Shu-Fang Chen, and Jun-Da Huang. "A Kinect-based system for physical rehabilitation: A pilot study for young adults with motor disabilities". In: *Res. Dev. Disabil.* 32.6 (2011), pp. 2566–2570.

[CG07]   Shi Chen and Youxing Gao. "An invariant appearance model for gait recognition". In: *Proc. IEEE Int. Conf. Multimed. and Expo (ICME)*. IEEE. 2007, pp. 1375–1378.

[Cha+06]   Yanmei Chai, Qing Wang, Jingping Jia, and Rongchun Zhao. "A novel human gait recognition method by segmenting and extracting the region variance feature". In: *Proc. Int. Conf. Pattern Recognit. (ICPR)*. Vol. 4. 2006, pp. 425–428.

[Cha+12]   Chien-Yen Chang et al. "Towards pervasive physical rehabilitation using Microsoft Kinect". In: *Proc. Int. Conf. Pervasive Comput. Technol. Healthc.* 2012, pp. 159–162.

[Che+09]   Changhong Chen, Jimin Liang, Heng Zhao, Haihong Hu, and Jie Tian. "Frame difference energy image for gait recognition with incomplete silhouettes". In: *Pattern Recognit. Lett.* 30.11 (2009), pp. 977–984.

[Che+11]   Bor-Rong Chen et al. "A Web-Based System for Home Monitoring of Patients With Parkinsonś Disease Using Wearable Sensors". In: *IEEE Trans. Biomed. Eng.* 58.3 (2011), pp. 831–836.

[Che+15]   Kun-Hui Chen, Po-Chao Chen, Kai-Chun Liu, and Chia-Tai Chan. "Wearable sensor-based rehabilitation exercise assessment for knee osteoarthritis". In: *Sensors* 15.2 (2015), pp. 4193–4211.

[Che+17a]   Chih-Chen Chen, Chun-Yen Liu, Shih-Hsiang Ciou, Shih-Ching Chen, and Yu-Luen Chen. "Digitized Hand Skateboard Based on IR-Camera for Upper Limb Rehabilitation". In: *J. Med. Syst.* 41.2 (2017).

[Che+17b]   Qiang Chen, Yunhong Wang, Zheng Liu, Qingjie Liu, and Di Huang. "Feature Map Pooling for Cross-View Gait Recognition Based on Silhouette Sequence Images". In: *arXiv preprint arXiv:1711.09358* (2017).

[CHE15]   M Eriksson Crommert, Kjartan Halvorsen, and Maria M Ekblom. "Trunk muscle activation at the initiation and braking of bilateral shoulder flexion movements of different amplitudes". In: *PloS one* 10.11 (2015), e0141777.

[Cho+14]   Benjamin Choo et al. "Statistical Analysis-Based Error Models for the Microsoft KinectTM Depth Sensor". In: *Sensors* 14.9 (2014), pp. 17430–17450.

[Cho+15]   Franccois Chollet et al. *Keras*. 2015.

[CK10]   Olivier Chapelle and S Sathiya Keerthi. "Efficient algorithms for ranking with SVMs". In: *Inf. Retr.* 13.3 (2010), pp. 201–215.

[CL11]   Chih-Chung Chang and Chih-Jen Lin. "LIBSVM: A library for support vector machines". In: *ACM Trans. Intell. Syst. Technol.(TIST)* 2 (2011), p. 27.

[CMJG16]   Francisco M Castro, Manuel J Marín-Jiménez, and Nicolás Guil. "Multimodal features fusion for gait, gender and shoes recognition". In: *Mach. Vis. Appl.* (2016), pp. 1–16.

[Cmu]   *CMU Motion Capture Database*. http://mocap.cs.cmu.edu/. [Online; accessed 01-April-2018].

[CNC03]   David Cunado, Mark S Nixon, and John N Carter. "Automatic extraction and description of human gait models for recognition purposes". In: *Comput. Vis. Image Underst.* 90.1 (2003), pp. 1–41.

[CT12]   Sruti Das Choudhury and Tardi Tjahjadi. "Silhouette-based gait recognition using Procrustes shape analysis and elliptic Fourier descriptors". In: *Pattern Recognit.* 45.9 (2012), pp. 3414–3426.

[DASZ09]   Farzin Dadashi, Babak N Araabi, and Hamid Soltanian-Zadeh. "Gait recognition using wavelet packet silhouette representation and transductive support vector machines". In: *IEEE Int. Cong. Image Signal Process. (CISP)*. 2009, pp. 1–5.

[DD]   Michael Doherty and John Doherty. *Clinical Examination in Rheumatology.* http://www.nle.nottingham.ac.uk/websites/rheumatology/. [Online; accessed 01-March-2018].

[Dd05]   Southampton Human ID at a Distance database. *Southampton Human ID at a Distance database.* http://www.gait.ecs.soton.ac.uk/database/. [Online; accessed 01-March-2018]. 2005.

[DG+12]   Alana Da Gama, Thiago Chaves, Lucas Figueiredo, and Veronica Teichrieb. "Guidance and movement correction based on therapeutics movements for motor rehabilitation support systems". In: *Symp. Virtual Augmented Real.* 2012, pp. 191–200.

[DG+15]   Alana Da Gama, Pascal Fallavollita, Veronica Teichrieb, and Nassir Navab. "Motor rehabilitation using Kinect: A systematic review". In: *Games Health J.* 4.2 (2015), pp. 123–135.

[DLR77]   Arthur P Dempster, Nan M Laird, and Donald B Rubin. "Maximum likelihood from incomplete data via the EM algorithm". In: *J. R. Stat. Soc. Ser. B-Stat. Methodol.* (1977), pp. 1–38.

[Dol+05]   Piotr Dollár et al. "Behavior recognition via sparse spatio-temporal features". In: *Int. Workshop Visual Surveill. Perform. Evaluation Track. Surveill.* IEEE. 2005, pp. 65–72.

[DR10]   Brian DeCann and Arun Ross. "Gait curves for human recognition, backpack detection, and silhouette correction in a nighttime environment". In: *SPIE Defense, Security, and Sensing*. 2010, 76670Q–76670Q.

[DSV13]   Yohan Dupuis, Xavier Savatier, and Pascal Vasseur. "Feature subset selection applied to model-free gait recognition". In: *Image Vis. Comput.* 31.8 (2013), pp. 580–591.

[DT05]   Navneet Dalal and Bill Triggs. "Histograms of oriented gradients for human detection". In: *Proc. IEEE Comput. Soc. Conf. Comput. Vis. Pattern Recognit. (CVPR)*. Vol. 1. IEEE. 2005, pp. 886–893.

[DTS06]   Navneet Dalal, Bill Triggs, and Cordelia Schmid. "Human detection using oriented histograms of flow and appearance". In: *ECCV*. Springer. 2006, pp. 428–441.

[Eve+11]   Lindsay Evett et al. "Dual Camera Motion Capture for Serious Games in Stroke Rehabilitation". In: *Proc. Int. Conf. Serious Games Appl. Health*. SEGAH '11. IEEE Computer Society, 2011, pp. 1–4. ISBN: 978-1-4673-0433-7.

[Exe+13]   Timothy Exell, Christopher Freeman, Katie Meadmore, Mustafa Kutlu, Eric Rogers, Ann-Marie Hughes, Emma Hallewell, and Jane Burridge. "Goal orientated stroke rehabilitation utilising electrical stimulation, iterative learning and microsoft kinect". In: *Proc. IEEE Int. Conf. Rehabil. Robot. (ICORR)*. 2013, pp. 1–6.

[Fan+08a]   Rong-En Fan, Kai-Wei Chang, Cho-Jui Hsieh, Xiang-Rui Wang, and Chih-Jen Lin. "LIBLINEAR: A library for large linear classification". In: *J. Mach. Learn. Res* 9.Aug (2008), pp. 1871–1874.

[Fan+08b]   Rong-En Fan, Kai-Wei Chang, Cho-Jui Hsieh, Xiang-Rui Wang, and Chih-Jen Lin. "LIBLINEAR: A library for large linear classification". In: *J. Mach. Learn. Res* 9.Aug (2008), pp. 1871–1874.

[FE73]   Martin A Fischler and Robert A Elschlager. "The representation and matching of pictorial structures". In: *IEEE Trans. Computer* 100.1 (1973), pp. 67–92.

[Fel+10]   Pedro F Felzenszwalb, Ross B Girshick, David McAllester, and Deva Ramanan. "Object detection with discriminatively trained part-based models". In: *IEEE Trans. Pattern Anal. Mach. Intell.* 32.9 (2010), pp. 1627–1645.

[Fis+13]   Nadine M Fisher, SC White, HJ Yack, RJ Smolinski, and DR Pendergast. *Effect of ACL Reconstruction and Gait Speed on Characteristics of Midstance and Stride Length.* https://sites.google.com/a/wfu.edu/aclgait/introduction. [Online; accessed 01-March-2018]. 2013.

[FT08]   Ali Farhadi and Mostafa Kamali Tabrizi. "Learning to recognize activities from the wrong view point". In: *ECCV*. Springer. 2008, pp. 154–166.

[GCN08]   Michela Goffredo, John N Carter, and Mark S Nixon. "Front-view gait recognition". In: *IEEE Int. Conf. Biometrics: Theory, Appl. Syst. (BTAS)*. IEEE. 2008, pp. 1–6.

[Gen+07]   Xin Geng et al. "Distance-driven fusion of gait and face for human identification in video". In: *Proc. Image Vis. Comput.* (2007).

[GGB84]   Arthur Goshtasby, Stuart H Gage, and Jon F Bartholic. "A Two-Stage Cross Correlation Approach to Template Matching". In: *IEEE Trans. Pattern Anal. Mach. Intell.* 6.3 (1984), pp. 374–378. ISSN: 0162-8828.

[GL13]   Yu Guan and Chang-Tsun Li. "A robust speed-invariant gait recognition system for walker and runner identification". In: *IEEE Int. Conf. Biometrics*. 2013, pp. 1–8.

[Gro+05]   Sabina E Groen, Alida CE De Blécourt, Klaas Postema, and Mijna Hadders-Algra. "General movements in early infancy predict neuromotor development at 9 to 12 years of age". In: *Developmental Med. Child Neurol.* 47.11 (2005), 731–738.

[GS01]   Ralph Gross and Jianbo Shi. *The cmu motion of body (mobo) database*. Carnegie Mellon University, 2001.

[GUQ13]   Cesar Guerrero and Alvaro Uribe-Quevedo. "Kinect-based posture tracking for correcting positions during exercise." In: *Studies in health technology and informatics* 184 (2013), pp. 158–160.

[Han+13]   Jungong Han, Ling Shao, Dong Xu, and Jamie Shotton. "Enhanced computer vision with microsoft kinect sensor: A review". In: *IEEE Trans. Cybern.* 43.5 (2013), pp. 1318–1334.

[HB06]   Jinguang Han and Bir Bhanu. "Individual recognition using gait energy image". In: *IEEE Trans. Pattern Anal. Mach. Intell.* 28.2 (2006), pp. 316–322.

[HBR12]   Martin Hofmann, Sebastian Bachmann, and Gerhard Rigoll. "2.5D gait biometrics using the depth gradient histogram energy image". In: *IEEE Int. Conf. Biometrics: Theory, Appl. Syst. (BTAS)*. 2012, pp. 399–403.

[Hei+10]   Franziska Heinze, Katharina Hesels, Nico Breitbach-Faller, Thomas Schmitz-Rode, and Catherine Disselhorst-Klug. "Movement analysis by accelerometry of newborns and infants for the early detection of movement disorders due to infantile cerebral palsy". In: *Med. Biol. Eng. Comput.* 48.8 (2010), pp. 765–772.

[Hes+06]   Todd Hester, Richard Hughes, Delsey M Sherrill, Bethany Knorr, Metin Akay, Joel Stein, and Paolo Bonato. "Using wearable sensors to measure motor abilities following stroke". In: *Int. Workshop Wearable Implantable Body Sensor Netw.* IEEE. 2006, 4–pp.

[Hes+15]   Nikolas Hesse, Gregor Stachowiak, Timo Breuer, and Michael Arens. "Estimating Body Pose of Infants in Depth Images Using Random Ferns". In: *Proc. IEEE Int. Conf. Comput. Vis. (ICCV)*. 2015.

[Hes+17]   Nikolas Hesse et al. "Body pose estimation in depth images for infant motion analysis". In: *Int. Conf. Eng. Med. Biol. Soc. (EMBC)*. IEEE. 2017, pp. 1909–1912.

[Hon+13]   Hossein Mousavi Hondori, Maryam Khademi, Lucy Dodakian, Steven C. Cramer, and Cristina Videira Lopes. "A spatial augmented reality rehab system for post-stroke hand rehabilitation". In: *MMVR*. 2013, pp. 279–285.

[Hu+13a]   Maodi Hu, Yunhong Wang, Zhaoxiang Zhang, De Zhang, and James J Little. "Incremental learning for video-based gait recognition with LBP flow". In: *IEEE Trans. Cybern.* 43.1 (2013), pp. 77–89.

[Hu+13b]   Maodi Hu, Yunhong Wang, Zhaoxiang Zhang, James J Little, and Di Huang. "View-invariant discriminative projection for multi-view gait-based human identification". In: *IEEE Trans. Inf. Forensics Security* 8.12 (2013), pp. 2034–2045.

[HU01]   HID-UMD. *University of Maryland Database (UMD)*. http://www.umiacs.umd.edu/labs/pirl/hid/data.html. [Online; accessed 01-March-2018]. 2001.

[Hu13]   Haifeng Hu. "Enhanced gabor feature based classification using a regularized locally tensor discriminant model for multiview gait recognition". In: *IEEE Trans. Circuits Syst. Video Technol.* 23.7 (2013), pp. 1274–1286.

[Hu14]   Haifeng Hu. "Multiview gait recognition based on patch distribution features and uncorrelated multilinear sparse local discriminant canonical correlation analysis". In: *IEEE Trans. Circuits Syst. Video Technol.* 24.4 (2014), pp. 617–630.

[Iwa+10]   Yumi Iwashita, Ryosuke Baba, Koichi Ogawara, and Ryo Kurazume. "Person identification from spatio-temporal 3D gait". In: *Int. Conf. Emerg. Secur. Technol. (EST)*. UK, 2010.

[Iwa+12]   Haruyuki Iwama, Mayu Okumura, Yasushi Makihara, and Yasushi Yagi. "The ou-isir gait database comprising the large population dataset and performance evaluation of gait recognition". In: *IEEE Trans. Inf. Forensics Security* 7.5 (2012), pp. 1511–1521.

[JBA09]   Frédéric Jean, Robert Bergevin, and Alexandra Branzan Albu. "Computing and evaluating view-normalized body part trajectories". In: *Image Vis. Comput.* 27.9 (2009), pp. 1272–1284.

[JH99]   Tommi Jaakkola and David Haussler. "Exploiting generative models in discriminative classifiers". In: *Advances in neural information processing systems*. 1999, pp. 487–493.

[Jun+17]   Michael Wilhelm Jung et al. "Vojta therapy and neurodevelopmental treatment in children with infantile postural asymmetry: a randomised controlled trial". In: *J. Phys. Ther. Sci.* 29.2 (2017), pp. 301–306.

[Kal+03]   Amir Kale, Naresh Cuntoor, B Yegnanarayana, AN Rajagopalan, and Ram Chellappa. "Gait analysis for human identification". In: *Int. Conf. Audio Video-Based Biometric Pers. Authentication*. Springer. 2003, pp. 706–714.

[Kal+04]   Amit Kale et al. "Identification of humans using gait". In: *IEEE Trans. Image Process.* 13.9 (2004), pp. 1163–1173.

[Kas+16]   Dimitris Kastaniotis, Ilias Theodorakopoulos, George Economou, and Spiros Fotopoulos. "Gait based recognition via fusing information from Euclidean and Riemannian manifolds". In: *Pattern Recognit. Lett.* 84 (2016), pp. 245–251.

[KCC03]   Amit Kale, Amit K Roy Chowdhury, and Rama Chellappa. "Towards a view invariant gait recognition algorithm". In: *IEEE Int. Conf. Adv. Video Signal-Based Surv. (AVSS)*. IEEE. 2003, pp. 143–150.

[Kus+09a]   Worapan Kusakunniran et al. "Automatic gait recognition using weighted binary pattern on video". In: *IEEE Int. Conf. Adv. Video Signal-Based Surv. (AVSS)*. IEEE. 2009, pp. 49–54.

[Kus+09b]   Worapan Kusakunniran, Qiang Wu, Hongdong Li, and Jian Zhang. "Multiple views gait recognition using view transformation model based on optimized gait energy image". In: *Proc. IEEE Int. Conf. Comput. Vis. (ICCV)*. IEEE. 2009, pp. 1058–1064.

[Kus+10]   Worapan Kusakunniran, Qiang Wu, Jian Zhang, and Hongdong Li. "Support vector regression for multi-view gait recognition based on local motion feature selection". In: *Proc. IEEE Comput. Soc. Conf. Comput. Vis. Pattern Recognit. (CVPR)*. IEEE. 2010, pp. 974–981.

[Kus+11a]   Worapan Kusakunniran, Qiang Wu, Jian Zhang, and Hongdong Li. "Pairwise shape configuration-based psa for gait recognition under small viewing angle change". In: *IEEE Int. Conf. Adv. Video Signal-Based Surv. (AVSS)*. IEEE. 2011, pp. 17–22.

[Kus+11b]   Worapan Kusakunniran, Qiang Wu, Jian Zhang, and Hongdong Li. "Speed-invariant gait recognition based on procrustes shape analysis using higher-order shape configuration". In: *Proc. Int. Conf. Image Process. (ICIP)*. 2011, pp. 545–548.

[Kus+12a]   Worapan Kusakunniran, Qiang Wu, Jian Zhang, and Hongdong Li. "Cross-view and multi-view gait recognitions based on view transformation model using multi-layer perceptron". In: *Pattern Recognit. Lett.* 33.7 (2012), pp. 882–889.

[Kus+12b]   Worapan Kusakunniran, Qiang Wu, Jian Zhang, and Hongdong Li. "Gait recognition across various walking speeds using higher order shape configuration based on a differential composition model". In: *IEEE Trans. Syst., Man, Cybern. B* 42.6 (2012), pp. 1654–1668.

[Kus+14]   Worapan Kusakunniran, Qiang Wu, Jian Zhang, Hongdong Li, and Liang Wang. "Recognizing gaits across views through correlated motion co-clustering". In: *IEEE Trans. Image Process.* 23.2 (2014), pp. 696–709.

[Kus14]   Worapan Kusakunniran. "Attribute-based learning for gait recognition using spatio-temporal interest points". In: *Image Vis. Comput.* 32.12 (2014), pp. 1117–1126.

[Lap05]   Ivan Laptev. "On space-time interest points". In: *Int. J. Comput. Vis.* 64.2-3 (2005), pp. 107–123.

[Lar+07]   Hugo Larochelle et al. "An empirical evaluation of deep architectures on problems with many factors of variation". In: *Int. Conf. Mach. Learn. (ICML)*. ACM. 2007, pp. 473–480.

[LB98]   James Little and Jeffrey Boyd. "Recognizing people by their gait: the shape of motion". In: *Videre: J. Comput. Vis. Res.* 1.2 (1998), pp. 1–32.

[LCL11]   Toby HW Lam, King Hong Cheung, and James NK Liu. "Gait flow image: A silhouette-based gait representation for human identification". In: *Pattern Recognit.* 44.4 (2011), pp. 973–987.

[Led+08]   Ron S Leder et al. "Nintendo Wii remote for computer simulated arm and wrist therapy in stroke survivors with upper extremity hemiparesis". In: *Virtual Rehabilitation.* IEEE. 2008, pp. 74–74.

[Lew95]   JP Lewis. "Fast Normalized Cross-Correlation". In: *Vision interface.* Vol. 10. 1995, pp. 120–123.

[LF+14]   David López-Fernández et al. "The AVA Multi-View Dataset for Gait Recognition". In: *Activity Monitoring by Multiple Distributed Sensing.* Springer International Publishing, 2014, pp. 26–39.

[LF+16]   David López-Fernández et al. "A new approach for multi-view gait recognition on unconstrained paths". In: *J. Vis. Commun. Image Represent.* 38 (2016), pp. 396–406.

[LG02]   Lily Lee and W Eric L Grimson. "Gait analysis for recognition and classification". In: *Int. Conf. Autom. Face Gesture Recognit.* IEEE. 2002, pp. 155–162.

[LHK08]   Heesung Lee, Sungjun Hong, and Euntai Kim. "An efficient gait recognition based on a selective neural network ensemble". In: *Int. J. Imaging Syst. Technol.* 18.4 (2008), pp. 237–241.

[Li+17]   Chao Li, Xin Min, Shouqian Sun, Wenqian Lin, and Zhichuan Tang. "Deepgait: a learning deep convolutional representation for view-invariant gait recognition using joint bayesian". In: *Applied Sci.* 7.3 (2017), p. 210.

[Lia+06]   Jimin Liang, Yan Chen, Haihong Hu, and Heng Zhao. "Appearance-based gait recognition using independent component analysis". In: *Int. Conf. Nat. Computation.* Springer. 2006, pp. 371–380.

[LLT11]   Nini Liu, Jiwen Lu, and Yap-Peng Tan. "Joint subspace learning for view-invariant gait recognition". In: *IEEE Signal Process. Lett.* 18.7 (2011), pp. 431–434.

[LO+13]   Laura Luna-Oliva et al. "Kinect Xbox 360 as a therapeutic modality for children with cerebral palsy in a school environment: a preliminary study". In: *NeuroRehab.* 33.4 (2013), pp. 513–521.

[LPV08]   Haiping Lu, Konstantinos N Plataniotis, and Anastasios N Venetsanopoulos. "A full-body layered deformable model for automatic model-based gait recognition". In: *EURASIP J. Adv. Signal Process.* 2008 (2008), p. 62.

[LSL08]   Peter K Larsen, Erik B Simonsen, and Niels Lynnerup. "Gait analysis in forensic medicine". In: *J. Forensic Sci.* 53.5 (2008), pp. 1149–1153.

[Lyo10]   Douglas Lyon. "The Discrete Fourier Transform, Part 6: Cross-Correlation". In: *J. Object Technol.* 9.2 (2010), pp. 18–22.

[LZJ06]   Jiwen Lu, Erhu Zhang, and Cuining Jing. "Gait recognition using wavelet descriptors and independent component analysis". In: *Int. Symp. Neural Netw.* Springer. 2006, pp. 232–237.

[Mak+06]   Yasushi Makihara, Ryusuke Sagawa, Yasuhiro Mukaigawa, Tomio Echigo, and Yasushi Yagi. "Gait recognition using a view transformation model in the frequency domain". In: *ECCV*. Springer. 2006, pp. 151–163.

[Mak+12]   Yasushi Makihara et al. "The OU-ISIR gait database comprising the treadmill dataset". In: *IPSJ Tran. Comput. Vis. Appl.* 4 (2012), pp. 53–62.

[Mak+15]   Yasushi Makihara et al. "Individuality-preserving silhouette extraction for gait recognition". In: *IPSJ Trans. on Comput. Vis. Appl.* 7 (2015), pp. 74–78.

[Man+00]   AJ Manson, P Brown, JD O'sullivan, P Asselman, D Buckwell, and AJ Lees. "An ambulatory dyskinesia monitor". In: *J. Neurol. Neurosurg. Psychiatry* 68.2 (2000), pp. 196–201.

[Man+14a] Al Mansur, Yasushi Makihara, Daigo Muramatsu, and Yasushi Yagi. "Cross-view gait recognition using view-dependent discriminative analysis". In: *Proc. Int. Joint Conf. Biometrics (IJCB)*. IEEE. 2014, pp. 1–8.

[Man+14b] Al Mansur, Yasushi Makihara, Rasyid Aqmar, and Yasush Yagi. "Gait recognition under speed transition". In: *Proc. IEEE Comput. Soc. Conf. Comput. Vis. Pattern Recognit. (CVPR)*. 2014, pp. 2521–2528.

[Mei+06]   L Meinecke, N Breitbach-Faller, C Bartz, R Damen, G Rau, and C Disselhorst-Klug. "Movement analysis in the early detection of newborns at risk for developing spasticity due to infantile cerebral palsy". In: *Human Mov. Sci.* 25.2 (2006), pp. 125 –144.

[MFX12]   Raúl Martín-Félez and Tao Xiang. "Gait recognition by ranking". In: *ECCV*. Springer. 2012, pp. 328–341.

[MHK14]   Hossein Mousavi Hondori and Maryam Khademi. "A Review on Technical and Clinical Impact of Microsoft Kinect on Physical Therapy and Rehabilitation". In: *J. Med. Informat.* (2014).

[MHN13]   Andrew L Maas, Awni Y Hannun, and Andrew Y Ng. "Rectifier nonlinearities improve neural network acoustic models". In: *Proc. icml*. Vol. 30. 2013, p. 3.

[Min96]   Jonathan W Mink. "THE BASAL GANGLIA: FOCUSED SELECTION AND INHIBITION OF COMPETING MOTOR PROGRAMS". In: *Prog. Neurobiol.* 50.4 (1996), pp. 381 –425.

[MMY16]   Daigo Muramatsu, Yasushi Makihara, and Yasushi Yagi. "View transformation model incorporating quality measures for cross-view gait recognition". In: *IEEE Trans. Cybern.* 46.7 (2016), pp. 1602–1615.

[Mur+12]   Daigo Muramatsu, Akira Shiraishi, Yasushi Makihara, and Yasushi Yagi. "Arbitrary view transformation model for gait person authentication". In: *IEEE Int. Conf. Biometrics: Theory, Appl. Syst. (BTAS)*. IEEE. 2012, pp. 85–90.

[Mur+15]   Daigo Muramatsu, Akira Shiraishi, Yasushi Makihara, Md Zasim Uddin, and Yasushi Yagi. "Gait-based person recognition using arbitrary view transformation model". In: *IEEE Trans. Image Process.* 24.1 (2015), pp. 140–154.

[Niz+08]   Imran Fareed Nizami et al. "Multi-view gait recognition fusion methodology". In: *IEEE Conf. Industrial Electronics Appl.* IEEE. 2008, pp. 2101–2105.

[NMY13]   Hozuma Nakajima, Ikuhisa Mitsugami, and Yasushi Yagi. "Depth-based gait feature representation". In: *IPSJ Tran. Comput. Vis. Appl.* 5 (2013), pp. 94–98.

[Nus12]   Henri J Nussbaumer. *Fast Fourier transform and convolution algorithms.* Vol. 2. Springer Science & Business Media, 2012.

[O'G03]   Lawrence O'Gorman. "Comparing passwords, tokens, and biometrics for user authentication". In: *Proc. IEEE* 91.12 (2003), pp. 2021–2040.

[oCo01]   GVU Center/College of Computing. *Georgia Tech. Database (GTD).* http://www.cc.gatech.edu/cpl/projects/hid/. [Online; accessed 01-March-2018]. 2001.

[Ols+14]   Mikkel Damgaard Olsen, Anna Herskind, Jens Bo Nielsen, and Rasmus Reinhold Paulsen. "Model-Based Motion Tracking of Infants." In: *ECCV Workshops (3).* 2014, pp. 673–685.

[Pal+16]   Federico Pala, Riccardo Satta, Giorgio Fumera, and Fabio Roli. "Multimodal person reidentification using RGB-D cameras". In: *IEEE Trans. Circuits Syst. Video Technol.* 26.4 (2016), pp. 788–799.

[Pao+14]   Gabriele Paolini, Agnese Peruzzi, Anat Mirelman, Andrea Cereatti, Stephen Gaukrodger, Jeffrey M Hausdorff, and Ugo Della Croce. "Validation of a method for real time foot position and orientation tracking with Microsoft Kinect technology for use in virtual reality and treadmill based gait training programs". In: *IEEE Trans. Neural Syst. Rehabil. Eng.* 22.5 (2014), pp. 997–1002.

[Pat+09]   Shyamal Patel et al. "Monitoring motor fluctuations in patients with Parkinson's disease using wearable sensors". In: *IEEE Trans. Inf. Technol. Biomed.* 13.6 (2009), pp. 864–873.

[PD13]   Benoit Penelle and Olivier Debeir. "Human motion tracking for rehabilitation using depth images and particle filter optimization". In: *Int. Conf. Adv. Biomed. Eng. (ICABME).* IEEE. 2013, pp. 211–214.

[Pen+14]   Xiaojiang Peng, Changqing Zou, Yu Qiao, and Qiang Peng. "Action recognition with stacked fisher vectors". In: *ECCV.* Springer. 2014, pp. 581–595.

[Pen+16]   Xiaojiang Peng, Limin Wang, Xingxing Wang, and Yu Qiao. "Bag of visual words and fusion methods for action recognition: Comprehensive study and good practice". In: *Comput. Vis. Image Underst.* 150 (2016), pp. 109 –125.

[Pie02]   Jan P Piek. "The role of variability in early motor development". In: *Infant Behav. Dev.* 25.4 (2002), pp. 452 –465.

[Pla]   *Plane Equation.* http://www.songho.ca/math/plane/plane.html. [Online; accessed 01-April-2018].

[PLC05]   Chulsung Park, Jinfeng Liu, and Pai H Chou. "Eco: An Ultra-compact Low-power Wireless Sensor Node for Real-time Motion Monitoring". In: *Proc. Int. Symp. Info. Process. Sens. Netw.* IPSN '05. IEEE Press, 2005. ISBN: 0-7803-9202-7.

[PP+16]   Jose Portillo-Portillo et al. "Cross View Gait Recognition Using Joint-Direct Linear Discriminant Analysis". In: *Sensors* 17.1 (2016), p. 6.

[Pra+11]   Sanjay K Prajapati, William H Gage, Dina Brooks, Sandra E Black, and William E McIlroy. "A novel approach to ambulatory monitoring: investigation into the quantity and control of everyday walking in patients with subacute stroke". In: *Neurorehabilit. Neural Repair* 25.1 (2011), pp. 6–14.

[Pre01]   Heinz FR Prechtl. "General movement assessment as a method of developmental neurology: new paradigms and their consequences The 1999 Ronnie MacKeith Lecture". In: *Developmental Med. Child Neurol.* 43.12 (2001), pp. 836–842.

[PSM10]   Florent Perronnin, Jorge Sánchez, and Thomas Mensink. "Improving the fisher kernel for large-scale image classification". In: *ECCV*. Springer. 2010, pp. 143–156.

[Rad+09]   Danny Rado, Aswin Sankaran, Joseph Plasek, David Nuckley, and Daniel F Keefe. "A Real-Time Physical Therapy Visualization Strategy to Improve Unsupervised Patient Rehabilitation". In: *IEEE Visualization*. 2009.

[Rah+14]   Hodjat Rahmati, Ole Morten Aamo, Øyvind Stavdahl, Ralf Dragon, and Lars Adde. "Video-based early cerebral palsy prediction using motion segmentation". In: *Int. Conf. Eng. Med. Biol. Soc. (EMBC)*. IEEE. 2014, pp. 3779–3783.

[Ram13]   Deva Ramanan. "Dual coordinate solvers for large-scale structural svms". In: *arXiv preprint arXiv:1312.1743* (2013).

[RJM16]   Imad Rida, Xudong Jiang, and Gian Luca Marcialis. "Human body part selection by group lasso of motion for model-free gait recognition". In: *IEEE Signal Process. Lett.* 23.1 (2016), pp. 154–158.

[RL14]   Neil T Roach and Daniel E Lieberman. "Upper body contributions to power generation during rapid, overhand throwing in humans". In: *J. Exp. Biol.* (2014), jeb–103275.

[RMS17]   Hossein Rahmani, Ajmal Mian, and Mubarak Shah. "Learning a deep model for human action recognition from novel viewpoints". In: *IEEE Trans. Pattern Anal. Mach. Intell.* (2017).

[Rou+07]   Caroline Rougier, Jean Meunier, Alain St-Arnaud, and Jacqueline Rousseau. "Fall detection from human shape and motion history using video surveillance". In: *IEEE Int. Conf. Adv. Inf. Netw. Appl. Workshops (AINAW)*. Vol. 2. IEEE. 2007, pp. 875–880.

[Sar+05]   Sudeep Sarkar et al. "The humanid gait challenge problem: Data sets, performance, and analysis". In: *IEEE Trans. Pattern Anal. Mach. Intell.* 27.2 (2005), pp. 162–177.

[SH06]   Han Su and Fenggang Huang. "Gait recognition using principal curves and neural networks". In: *Int. Symp. Neural Netw.* Springer. 2006, pp. 238–243.

[Shi+16]   Kohei Shiraga, Yasushi Makihara, Daigo Muramatsu, Tomio Echigo, and Yasushi Yagi. "Geinet: View-invariant gait recognition using a convolutional neural network". In: *IEEE Int. Conf. Biometrics*. IEEE. 2016, pp. 1–8.

[Sho+13]   Jamie Shotton et al. "Real-time human pose recognition in parts from single depth images". In: *Communications of the ACM* 56.1 (2013), pp. 116–124.

[Siv+11a] Sabesan Sivapalan, Daniel Chen, Simon Denman, Sridha Sridharan, and Clinton Fookes. "3D ellipsoid fitting for multi-view gait recognition". In: *IEEE Int. Conf. Adv. Video Signal-Based Surv. (AVSS)*. IEEE. 2011, pp. 355–360.

[Siv+11b] Sabesan Sivapalan, Daniel Chen, Simon Denman, Sridha Sridharan, and Clinton Fookes. "Gait energy volumes and frontal gait recognition using depth images". In: *Proc. Int. Joint Conf. Biometrics (IJCB)*. 2011, pp. 1–6.

[Siv+13]   Sabesan Sivapalan, Daniel Chen, Simon Denman, Sridha Sridharan, and Clinton Fookes. "Histogram of weighted local directions for gait recognition". In: *Proc. IEEE Comput. Soc. Conf. Comput. Vis. Pattern Recognit. (CVPR)*. 2013, pp. 125–130.

[Soi13]   Pierre Soille. *Morphological image analysis: principles and applications*. Springer Science & Business Media, 2013.

[SSC14]   Soharab Hossain Shaikh, Khalid Saeed, and Nabendu Chaki. "Gait recognition using partial silhouette-based approach". In: *Int. Conf. Signal Process. Integr. Netw. (SPIN)*. IEEE. 2014, pp. 101–106.

[Sta+12]   Annette Stahl, Christian Schellewald, Øyvind Stavdahl, Ole Morten Aamo, Lars Adde, and Harald Kirkerod. "An optical flow-based method to predict infantile cerebral palsy". In: *IEEE Trans. Neural Syst. Rehabil. Eng.* 20.4 (2012), pp. 605–614.

[Sán+13]   Jorge Sánchez, Florent Perronnin, Thomas Mensink, and Jakob Verbeek. "Image classification with the fisher vector: Theory and practice". In: *Int. J. Comput. Vis.* 105.3 (2013), pp. 222–245.

[Tan+06]   Daoliang Tan, Kaiqi Huang, Shiqi Yu, and Tieniu Tan. "Efficient night gait recognition based on template matching". In: *Proc. Int. Conf. Pattern Recognit. (ICPR)*. Vol. 3. 2006, pp. 1000–1003.

[Tan+07a] Daoliang Tan, Kaiqi Huang, Shiqi Yu, and Tieniu Tan. "Orthogonal diagonal projections for gait recognition". In: *Proc. Int. Conf. Image Process. (ICIP)*. Vol. 1. IEEE. 2007, pp. I–337.

[Tan+07b] Daoliang Tan, Kaiqi Huang, Shiqi Yu, and Tieniu Tan. "Recognizing night walkers based on one pseudoshape representation of gait". In: *Proc. IEEE Comput. Soc. Conf. Comput. Vis. Pattern Recognit. (CVPR)*. IEEE. 2007, pp. 1–8.

[Tan+07c] Daoliang Tan, Kaiqi Huang, Shiqi Yu, and Tieniu Tan. "Uniprojective features for gait recognition". In: *Proc. Int. Conf. Biometrics*. Springer. 2007, pp. 673–682.

[Tan+07d] Daoliang Tan, Shiqi Yu, Kaiqi Huang, and Tieniu Tan. "Walker recognition without gait cycle estimation". In: *Proc. Int. Conf. Biometrics*. 2007, pp. 222–231.

[Tan+17]   Jin Tang, Jian Luo, Tardi Tjahjadi, and Fan Guo. "Robust arbitrary-view gait recognition based on 3d partial similarity matching". In: *IEEE Trans. Image Process.* 26.1 (2017), pp. 7–22.

[TH04]   Yaqin Tao and Huosheng Hu. "Colour based human motion tracking for home-based rehabilitation". In: *Int. Conf. Syst. Man Cybern.* Vol. 1. IEEE. 2004, pp. 773–778.

[TH12]   Tijmen Tieleman and Geoffrey Hinton. "Lecture 6.5-rmsprop: Divide the gradient by a running average of its recent magnitude". In: *COURSERA: Neural networks for machine learning* 4.2 (2012), pp. 26–31.

[TK09]   Sergios Theodoridis and Konstantinos Koutroumbas. *Pattern Recognition.* Elsevier, 2009.

[Tse+09]   Yu-Chee Tseng et al. "A wireless human motion capturing system for home rehabilitation". In: *Int. Conf. Mob. Data Manage.: Syst. Serv. Middlew. (MDM).* IEEE. 2009, pp. 359–360.

[Tso+04]   Ioannis Tsochantaridis, Thomas Hofmann, Thorsten Joachims, and Yasemin Altun. "Support vector machine learning for interdependent and structured output spaces". In: *Int. Conf. Mach. Learn. (ICML).* ACM. 2004, p. 104.

[VCC04]   Ashok Veeraraghavan, A Roy Chowdhury, and Rama Chellappa. "Role of shape and kinematics in human movement analysis". In: *Proc. IEEE Comput. Soc. Conf. Comput. Vis. Pattern Recognit. (CVPR).* Vol. 1. IEEE. 2004, pp. I–730.

[VJ01]   Paul Viola and Michael Jones. "Rapid object detection using a boosted cascade of simple features". In: *Proc. IEEE Comput. Soc. Conf. Comput. Vis. Pattern Recognit. (CVPR).* Vol. 1. IEEE. 2001, pp. I–I.

[VRCC05]   Ashok Veeraraghavan, Amit K Roy-Chowdhury, and Rama Chellappa. "Matching shape sequences in video with applications in human movement analysis". In: *IEEE Trans. Pattern Anal. Mach. Intell.* 27.12 (2005), pp. 1896–1909.

[Wan+03a] Liang Wang, Tieniu Tan, Weiming Hu, Huazhong Ning, et al. "Automatic gait recognition based on statistical shape analysis". In: *IEEE Trans. Image Process.* 12.9 (2003), pp. 1120–1131.

[Wan+03b] Liang Wang, Tieniu Tan, Huazhong Ning, and Weiming Hu. "Silhouette analysis-based gait recognition for human identification". In: *IEEE Trans. Pattern Anal. Mach. Intell.* 25.12 (2003), pp. 1505–1518.

[Wan+04]   Liang Wang, Huazhong Ning, Tieniu Tan, and Weiming Hu. "Fusion of static and dynamic body biometrics for gait recognition". In: *IEEE Trans. Circuits Syst. Video Technol.* 14.2 (2004), pp. 149–158.

[Wan+12]   Chen Wang, Junping Zhang, Liang Wang, Jian Pu, and Xiaoru Yuan. "Human identification using temporal information preserving gait template". In: *IEEE Trans. Pattern Anal. Mach. Intell.* 34.11 (2012), pp. 2164–2176.

[Wan+13]   Heng Wang et al. "Dense trajectories and motion boundary descriptors for action recognition". In: *Int. J. Comput. Vis.* 103.1 (2013), pp. 60–79.

[Wan+15]   Qi Wang, Wei Chen, Annick AA Timmermans, Christoforos Karachristos, Jean-Bernard Martens, and Panos Markopoulos. "Smart Rehabilitation Garment for posture monitoring". In: *Int. Conf. Eng. Med. Biol. Soc. (EMBC).* IEEE. 2015, pp. 5736–5739.

[WBR14] Tenika Whytock, Alexander Belyaev, and Neil M Robertson. "Dynamic distance-based shape features for gait recognition". In: *J. Math. Imaging Vis.* 50.3 (2014), pp. 314–326.

[WRB06] Daniel Weinland, Remi Ronfard, and Edmond Boyer. "Free viewpoint action recognition using motion history volumes". In: *Comput. Vis. Image Underst.* 104.2-3 (2006), pp. 249–257.

[WS13] Heng Wang and Cordelia Schmid. "Action recognition with improved trajectories". In: *Proc. IEEE Int. Conf. Comput. Vis. (ICCV)*. 2013, pp. 3551–3558.

[Wu+07] Qiang Wu et al. "Dynamic biometrics fusion at feature level for video based human recognition". In: *Proc. Image Vis. Comput.* Citeseer. 2007, pp. 152–157.

[Wu+17] Zifeng Wu, Yongzhen Huang, Liang Wang, Xiaogang Wang, and Tieniu Tan. "A comprehensive study on cross-view gait based human identification with deep cnns". In: *IEEE Trans. Pattern Anal. Mach. Intell.* 39.2 (2017), pp. 209–226.

[Wu11] KK Wu. "Using Human Skeleton to Recognizing Human Exercise by Kinect's Camera". In: *Master, Department of Computer Science and Information Engineering, National Taipei University of Technology* (2011).

[XCA11] Lu Xia, Chia-Chih Chen, and Jake K Aggarwal. "Human detection using depth information by Kinect". In: *Proc. IEEE Comput. Soc. Conf. Comput. Vis. Pattern Recognit. Workshop (CVPRW)*. 2011, pp. 15–22.

[YNC02] ChewYean Yam, Mark S Nixon, and John N Carter. "Gait recognition by walking and running: a model-based approach". In: *Asian Conf. Comput. Vis. (ACCV)*. 2002, pp. 1–6.

[YR13] Yi Yang and Deva Ramanan. "Articulated human detection with flexible mixtures of parts". In: *IEEE Trans. Pattern Anal. Mach. Intell.* 35.12 (2013), pp. 2878–2890.

[YTL14] Yazhou Yang, Dan Tu, and Guohui Li. "Gait Recognition Using Flow Histogram Energy Image". In: *Proc. Int. Conf. Pattern Recognit. (ICPR)*. 2014, pp. 444–449.

[YTT06] Shiqi Yu, Daoliang Tan, and Tieniu Tan. "A framework for evaluating the effect of view angle, clothing and carrying condition on gait recognition". In: *Proc. Int. Conf. Pattern Recognit. (ICPR)*. Vol. 4. IEEE. 2006, pp. 441–444.

[Yu+06] Shiqi Yu et al. "A framework for evaluating the effect of view angle, clothing and carrying condition on gait recognition". In: *Proc. Int. Conf. Pattern Recognit. (ICPR)*. Vol. 4. 2006, pp. 441–444.

[YXL14] Li Yao, Hui Xu, and Andong Li. "Kinect-based rehabilitation exercises system: therapist involved approach". In: *Biomed. Mater. Eng.* 24.6 (2014), pp. 2611–2618.

[YZC15] Chao Yan, Bailing Zhang, and Frans Coenen. "Multi-attributes gait identification by convolutional neural networks". In: *IEEE Int. Cong. Image Signal Process. (CISP)*. IEEE. 2015, pp. 642–647.

[Zha+06]   Guoying Zhao, Guoyi Liu, Hua Li, and Matti Pietikainen. "3D gait recognition using multiple cameras". In: *Int. Conf. Autom. Face Gesture Recognit.* IEEE. 2006, pp. 529–534.

[Zha+17]   Zhaoxiang Zhang, Jiaxin Chen, Qiang Wu, and Ling Shao. "GII Representation-Based Cross-View Gait Recognition by Discriminative Projection With List-Wise Constraints". In: *IEEE Trans. Cybern.* (2017).

[Zha12]   David D Zhang. *Biometric solutions: For authentication in an e-world.* Vol. 697. Springer Science & Business Media, 2012.

[Zhe+11]   Shuai Zheng, Junge Zhang, Kaiqi Huang, Ran He, and Tieniu Tan. "Robust view transformation model for gait recognition". In: *Proc. Int. Conf. Image Process. (ICIP).* IEEE. 2011, pp. 2073–2076.

[Zhe+12]   Shuai Zheng, Kaiqi Huang, Tieniu Tan, and Dacheng Tao. "A cascade fusion scheme for gait and cumulative foot pressure image recognition". In: *Pattern Recognit.* 45.10 (2012), pp. 3603–3610.

[ZT05]   Zonghua Zhang and Nikolaus F Troje. "View-independent person identification from human gait". In: *Neurocomputing* 69.1-3 (2005), pp. 250–256.

[ZTB16]   Wenlong Zhang, Masayoshi Tomizuka, and Nancy Byl. "A wireless human motion monitoring system for smart rehabilitation". In: *J. Dyn. Syst. Measurement Control* 138.11 (2016), p. 111004.

[ZWY14]   Wei Zeng, Cong Wang, and Feifei Yang. "Silhouette-based gait recognition via deterministic learning". In: *Pattern Recognit.* 47.11 (2014), pp. 3568–3584.

[ZZX10]   Erhu Zhang, Yongwei Zhao, and Wei Xiong. "Active energy image plus 2DLPP for gait recognition". In: *Signal Process.* 90.7 (2010), pp. 2295–2302.

Own Publications

[Del+17]   Ahmad Delforouzi, Amir Hossein Tabatabaei, Muhammad Hassan Khan, and Marcin Grzegorzek. "A Vision-Based Method for Automatic Crack Detection in Railway Sleepers". In: *Proc. Int. Conf. Comput. Recognit. Systems (CORES)*. Springer. 2017, pp. 130–139.

[Far+17]   Muhammad Shahid Farid, Maurizio Lucenteforte, Muhammad Hassan Khan, and Marco Grangetto. "Semi-automatic Segmentation of Scattered and Distributed Objects". In: *Proc. Int. Conf. Comput. Recognit. Systems (CORES)*. Springer. 2017, pp. 110–119.

[KFG17]   Muhammad Hassan Khan, Muhammad Shahid Farid, and Marcin Grzegorzek. "Person Identification Using Spatiotemporal Motion Characteristics". In: *Proc. Int. Conf. Image Process. (ICIP)*. IEEE. 2017, pp. 166–170.

[KFG18a]   Muhammad Hassan Khan, Muhammad Shahid Farid, and Marcin Grzegorzek. "Spatiotemporal Feature of Human Motion for Gait Recognition". In: *Signal Image Video Process.* (2018). **[Impact Factor: 1.64]**.

[KFG18b]   Muhammad Hassan Khan, Muhammad Shahid Farid, and Marcin Grzegorzek. "Using a Generic Model for Codebook-based Gait Recognition Algorithms". In: *IEEE Int. Workshop Biometrics Forensics (IWBF)* (2018).

[KG17]   Muhammad Hassan Khan and Marcin Grzegorzek. "Vojta Therapy: A Vision-Based Framework to Recognize the Movement Patterns". In: *Int. J. Softw. Innovat.* 5.3 (2017), pp. 18–32.

[Kha+16a]   Muhammad Hassan Khan, Julien Helsper, Cong Yang, and Marcin Grzegorzek. "An automatic vision-based monitoring system for accurate Vojtatherapy". In: *IEEE Int. Conf. Comput. Inf. Sci. (ICIS)*. IEEE. 2016, pp. 1–6.

[Kha+16b]   Muhammad Hassan Khan, Jullien Helsper, Zeyd Boukhers, and Marcin Grzegorzek. "Automatic recognition of movement patterns in the vojtatherapy using RGB-D data". In: *Proc. Int. Conf. Image Process. (ICIP)*. IEEE. 2016, pp. 1235–1239.

[Kha+16c]   Muhammad Hassan Khan, Kimiaki Shirahama, Muhammad Shahid Farid, and Marcin Grzegorzek. "Multiple human detection in depth images". In: *Proc. Int. Workshop Multimed. Signal Process. (MMSP)*. IEEE. 2016, pp. 1–6.

[Kha+17]   Muhammad Hassan Khan, Frederic Li, Muhammad Shahid Farid, and Marcin Grzegorzek. "Gait recognition using motion trajectory analysis". In: *Proc. Int. Conf. Comput. Recognit. Systems (CORES)*. Springer. 2017, pp. 73–82.

[Kha+18a] Muhammad Hassan Khan, Julien Helsper, Muhammad Shahid Farid, and Marcin Grzegorzek. "A computer vision-based system for monitoring Vojta therapy". In: *J. Med. Informat.* 113 (2018), pp. 85–95. **[Impact Factor: 3.21]**.

[Kha+18b] Muhammad Hassan Khan, Muhammad Shahid Farid, Mariyam Zahoor, and Marcin Grzegorzek. "Cross-view Gait Recognition using Non-linear View Transformations of Spatiotemporal Features". In: *Proc. Int. Conf. Image Process. (ICIP)*. IEEE. 2018.

[Kha+18c] Muhammad Hassan Khan, Manuel Schneider, Muhammad Shahid Farid, and Marcin Grzegorzek. "Detection of Infantile Movement Disorders in Video Data Using Deformable Part-Based Model". In: *Sensors* 18 (2018). **[Impact Factor: 2.48]**.

[Tie+16] Oliver Tiebe, Cong Yang, Muhammad Hassan Khan, Marcin Grzegorzek, and Dominik Scarpin. "Stripes-Based Object Matching". In: *Computer and Information Science*. Springer, 2016, pp. 59–72.

In der Reihe *Studien zur Mustererkennung,*
herausgegeben von
Prof. Dr. Ing Heinricht Niemann und Herrn Prof. Dr. Ing. Elmar Nöth
sind bisher erschienen:

1   Jürgen Haas   Probabilistic Methods in Linguistic Analysis

                            ISBN 978-3-89722-565-7, 2000, 260 S.   40.50 €

2   Manuela Boros   Partielles robustes Parsing spontansprachlicher
                            Dialoge am Beispiel von Zugauskunftdialogen

                            ISBN 978-3-89722-600-5, 2001, 264 S.   40.50 €

3   Stefan Harbeck   Automatische Verfahren zur Sprachdetektion,
                            Landessprachenerkennung und Themendetektion

                            ISBN 978-3-89722-766-8, 2001, 260 S.   40.50 €

4   Julia Fischer   Ein echtzeitfähiges Dialogsystem mit iterativer
                            Ergebnisoptimierung

                            ISBN 978-3-89722-867-2, 2002, 222 S.   40.50 €

5   Ulrike Ahlrichs   Wissensbasierte Szenenexploration auf der Basis
                            erlernter Analysestrategien

                            ISBN 978-3-89722-904-4, 2002, 165 S.   40.50 €

6   Florian Gallwitz   Integrated Stochastic Models for Spontaneous
                            Speech Recognition

                            ISBN 978-3-89722-907-5, 2002, 196 S.   40.50 €

7   Uwe Ohler   Computational Promoter Recognition in
                            Eukaryotic Genomic DNA

                            ISBN 978-3-89722-988-4, 2002, 206 S.   40.50 €

8   Richard Huber   Prosodisch-linguistische Klassifikation
                            von Emotion

                            ISBN 978-3-89722-984-6, 2002, 293 S.   40.50 €

9	Volker Warnke	Integrierte Segmentierung und Klassifikation von Äußerungen und Dialogakten mit heterogenen Wissensquellen
		ISBN 978-3-8325-0254-6, 2003, 182 S. 40.50 €
10	Michael Reinhold	Robuste, probabilistische, erscheinungsbasierte Objekterkennung
		ISBN 978-3-8325-0476-2, 2004, 283 S. 40.50 €
11	Matthias Zobel	Optimale Brennweitenwahl für die multiokulare Objektverfolgung
		ISBN 978-3-8325-0496-0, 2004, 292 S. 40.50 €
12	Bernd Ludwig	Ein konfigurierbares Dialogsystem für Mensch-Maschine-Interaktion in gesprochener Sprache
		ISBN 978-3-8325-0497-7, 2004, 230 S. 40.50 €
13	Rainer Deventer	Modeling and Control of Static and Dynamic Systems with Bayesian Networks
		ISBN 978-3-8325-0521-9, 2004, 195 S. 40.50 €
14	Jan Buckow	Multilingual Prosody in Automatic Speech Understanding
		ISBN 978-3-8325-0581-3, 2004, 164 S. 40.50 €
15	Klaus Donath	Automatische Segmentierung und Analyse von Blutgefäßen
		ISBN 978-3-8325-0642-1, 2004, 210 S. 40.50 €
16	Axel Walthelm	Sensorbasierte Lokalisations-Algorithmen für mobile Service-Roboter
		ISBN 978-3-8325-0691-9, 2004, 200 S. 40.50 €
17	Ricarda Dormeyer	Syntaxanalyse auf der Basis der Dependenzgrammatik
		ISBN 978-3-8325-0723-7, 2004, 200 S. 40.50 €
18	Michael Levit	Spoken Language Understanding without Transcriptions in a Call Center Scenario
		ISBN 978-3-8325-0930-9, 2005, 249 S. 40.50 €

39	Chen Li	Content-based Microscopic Image Analysis	
		ISBN 978-3-8325-4253-5, 2016, 196 S.	36.50 €
40	Christian Feinen	Object Representation and Matching Based on Skeletons and Curves	
		ISBN 978-3-8325-4257-3, 2016, 260 S.	50.50 €
41	Juan Rafael Orozco-Arroyave	Analysis of Speech of People with Parkinson's Disease	
		ISBN 978-3-8325-4361-7, 2016, 138 S.	38.00 €
42	Cong Yang	Object Shape Generation, Representation and Matching	
		ISBN 978-3-8325-4399-0, 2016, 194 S.	36.50 €
43	Florian Hönig	Automatic Assessment of Prosody in Second Language Learning	
		ISBN 978-3-8325-4567-3, 2017, 256 S.	38.50 €
44	Zeyd Boukhers	3D Trajectory Extraction from 2D Videos for Human Activity Analysis	
		ISBN 978-3-8325-4583-3, 2017, 152 S.	35.00 €
45	Muhammad Hassan Khan	Human Activity Analysis in Visual Surveillance and Healthcare	
		ISBN 978-3-8325-4807-0, 2017, 156 S.	35.00 €

Alle erschienenen Bücher können unter der angegebenen ISBN im Buchhandel oder direkt beim Logos Verlag Berlin (www.logos-verlag.de, Fax: 030 - 42 85 10 92) bestellt werden.